THE BEACHES OF THE
D-DAY LANDINGS

TEXT
YVES LECOUTURIER

TRANSLATION
ENTREPRISES 35

D0474334

Éditions Ouest-France

MEMORIAL
CAEN NORMANDIE

NORMANDIE
TERRE-LIBERTÉ

"Passer-by, stop and meditate"
(MEMORIAL STONE AT LUC-SUR-MER)

CONTENTS

UNITED WE WIN

The preparations

In the summer of 1940, by creating a joint operations command, the British Prime Minister Winston Churchill demonstrated his determination to continue the fight and to take an active part in the liberation of Europe. Roosevelt and Churchill met a first time in New-foundland in August 1941 and concluded the Atlantic Charter. A few days after the Japanese raid on Pearl Harbour in December 1941, Roosevelt and Churchill met again in order to work out a common strategy against the Axis powers and in particular against Germany. The Washington conference decided to create a joint general staff, the Combined Chiefs of Staff. On January 24th 1943, Roosevelt, Churchill, de Gaulle and General Giraud met in Casablanca with their chiefs of staff and decided to launch the landings on the north-west coast of Europe to defeat Germany: *"The war will continue until the complete and unconditional surrender of the foe"*. This decision was accompanied by the creation of a joint inter-arm general staff or COSSAC: Chief of Staff of the Supreme Allied Commander. This task, assigned to the British General Frederick Morgan on March 12th 1943, comprised a vast amphibious operation to establish a bridgehead on the continent and to develop a decisive attack aimed at

The Casablanca Conference, January 24th 1943.

Germany. British and American officers began to work together and on March 28th they met secretly in Scotland.

There were three methods of attack: Starkey, a diversion operation in 1943, Rankin, an attack ready at any moment if Germany collapsed, and Overlord, the landings operation of May 1944. The choice of the landing site favoured Normandy for meteorological and wind conditions, and also because the beaches were easily accessible and poorly defended. Since 1941, British commandos had worked mainly on the Calvados shores: Luc-sur-Mer on September 28th 1941,

Left:
American propaganda poster.

5

The Allied general staff: seated, from left to right: Tedder, Eisenhower, Montgomery, standing, from left to right: Bradley, Ramsay, Leigh-Mallory, Bedell-Smith.

Model of Pegasus Bridge.

Saint-Aubin-sur-Mer during the night of September 27th to 28th of the same year and Saint-Laurent-sur-Mer during the night of January 17th to 18th 1942. These were mainly reconnaissance raids. On August 19th, Lord Louis Mountbatten, cousin of King George VIth, in charge of the joint operations, launched the 2nd Canadian division on the German defences in Dieppe, but Operation Jubilee was a total failure; more than 4,300 men were killed, wounded or missing. Nonetheless, the Allies were able to learn from this for future landings on the Normandy coast. The same year, 1942, General George Marshall drew up the Round-Up landing plan for the allies on the Channel beaches, but the British considered this to be premature. In May 1943, the Washington Trident conference adapted the main points of this plan which became Operation Overlord: it was approved in August at the Quebec Quadrant conference and planned for the month of May 1944. The COSSAC thus became an operational entity. Landing operations followed one after the other and were improved: Torch in North Africa on November 8th 1942, Husky in Sicily on July 10th 1943, and the Anzio landing in January 1944. By

November 1943, four American divisions and three British divisions, all experienced, were moved from Italy and Africa. In December 1943, the Overlord supreme command (SHAEF: Supreme Headquarters Allied Expeditionary Forces) was awarded to General Dwight Eisenhower. He appointed Sir Arthur Tedder as his second-in-command, Bertram Ramsay to supervise maritime operations, Trafford Leigh-Mallory for air operations, while Walter Bedell-Smith was made his chief of staff. Land forces were confided jointly to Omar Bradley and Bernard Montgomery. In January 1944, Eisenhower

was given the following mission; "*You will enter the continent of Europe and, in conjunction with the other united nations, undertake operations aimed at the heart of Germany and the destruction of her armed forces*". In February 1944, he confided to Sir Bernard Montgomery that the plan for the landings needed to be revised: the front was widened from 25 to 50 miles, from the estuary of the river Orne (Calvados) to the Varreville dunes (Manche) and was to be attacked by five infantry divisions and three airborne divisions. At the same time, the date for the landing operations on the Côte d'Azur was changed to August 15th.

Since the failure of the Jubilee operation in the port of Dieppe there was no longer any question of attacking a port directly. The Allies therefore decided to adopt an idea of Winston Churchill to build an artificial port to disembark men, equipment and supplies: the port was to be prefabricated in England then convoyed across the Channel and assembled in situ. Twenty thousand workers were to manufacture the elements for the artificial port in a few months. Then there was the question of finding a solution to all the logistical problems posed by the landings, for example sending fuel across from the Isle of Wight to Cherbourg or the amphibious tanks. Ships were needed to transport soldiers and equipment. The whole of the south of England became one gigantic

military camp firmly isolated from the surrounding population. The soldiers practised many exercises. For example, in May 1944, the Fabius exercise took place in Slapton Sands in Devon: the assault troops of the 1st and 2nd American divisions carried out an amphibious landing as a rehearsal of the framework of Operation Overlord. These exercises proved to be disastrous, with over 900 deaths.

The British paratroopers of the airborne forces repeated the taking of the Bénouville Bridge time and time again, until they knew the smallest details of the terrain.

There were three conditions needed to set the landing day: a high half-tide for the ships, a dawn assault and a full moon at night for the airborne troops, but these factors only coincided

Fabius exercise, Slapton Sands, Devon, May 1944.

Fabius exercise, rehearsal of Operation Overlord.

Canadian troops boarding.

several times a month: in June 1944 the days were the 5th, 6th and 7th. On May 17th, Eisenhower set the date for Monday June 5th, with a possible delay to the Tuesday or Wednesday.

The Allies prepared the landings down to the minutest detail since the liberation of Europe was at stake. If they were to succeed, they had to assert themselves quickly over the Germans through joint sea and air control. In 1943, American factories produced 30,000 tanks and 86,000 planes. All were sent to England on Liberty ships whereas the men, about 150,000 each month, travelled in steamers. At the beginning of spring, all the means of road and rail communication were systematically bombed in order to isolate the north-west of France. From the month of April, all the coastal defences of the Atlantic Wall were targeted. In June 1944, Allied airborne forces (British Bomber Command and American Strategic Air Force) had more than 11,000 planes including 3,500 fighter planes and

after May 1943 when Admiral Doenitz decided to withdraw from the Atlantic Ocean. The battle of the Atlantic began in 1939, but became fiercer in 1940 when the Germans took the French ports. Until May 1943, German submarines ruled the ocean: between May and August, 97 submarines were sunk. On their side, the Allies mobilised everything which could float. On D-Day, each of the 187 Allied warships was given a very precise target. Apart from this mastery of the sea, the airspace was also under control, making it possible to fly in to bomb and pound Germany, but also France where the targets were the Atlantic Wall, radar stations, bridges and railway lines. In total, nearly 80,000 tons of bombs were dropped in the two months preceding the landings.

By the eve of June 6th, 1.7 million Americans had arrived. In total, the Allied armies comprised nearly 3 million soldiers spread over 39 divisions: 20 American, 14 British, 3 Canadian, 1 Polish and 1 French. A million men came from the Commonwealth. The rest comprised French, Belgian, Norwegian, Polish, Czech and Dutch formations.

The Allies tried to trick the Germans about their intentions by organising Operation Bodyguard, to make them think that landings would take place after the month of July and in a site which had not yet been decided. Among the hoaxes, the most remarkable was Operation Fortitude. It consisted of convincing the Germans that the bridgehead for an Allied landing would be in the Pas-de-Calais. In order to do this, a ghost army was created from nothing, comprising decoys with for example decors in cardboard or rubber blow-up Jeeps and armoured vehicles. To complete the brainwashing, leaks were given to the press, but above all this phantom army was put under the command of George Patton. The spies of the IIIrd Reich confirmed these dummy preparations. Despite several minor

5,000 bombers while the Germans only had 500 planes. On D-Day, the Allied planes carried out almost 15,000 sorties whereas the Luftwaffe could only carry out 300! Thus it was almost absent from the landing beaches. In his book "The US Army Air Force in the Second World War", John Flag writes: *"The Anglo-American air forces did more than just support the historic invasion of June 6th 1944; they made it possible".*

This airborne superiority was backed up by control of the seas

*German sentry
on the Atlantic Wall.*

incidents, the great D-Day secret was kept until the end.

The French and Belgian resistants were and remained mobilised to find information about all the German dispositions, their positions and above all the movement of units. All this information beginning with the theft of the Atlantic Wall map in May 1942 by a resistant, was a great help in preparing Operation Overlord. Apart from the presence of the 352nd German infantry division, which came to Bessin for manoeuvres, the Allies knew exactly where all the others were stationed.

The Normans were not unaware that a landing could take place on their coasts. There were more and more evacuations in 1943 and 1944. In 1943 Cherbourg, transformed into a fortress, saw the major part of its population evacuated to the south of the département. The Bessin coast and zone from Cabourg to Honfleur saw the same in May 1944. The idea of landings had entered the minds of the Normans. In January 1944, a report from French

general intelligence noted that "*everyone is expecting important things to happen*". The landings were expected in the middle of March, and then in April, but in vain. The many German preparations and the intensified bombing led the French authorities to think that the landings were close. As a result, on April 25th 1944, the sub-prefect of Vire noted that: "*The Anglo-American landings, considered to be imminent, are the order of the day*". Joseph Poirier witnessed this state of mind of many Normans in the spring of 1944: "*We knew very well that delivery was close, that liberation was sounding, but as egoists we thought that the*

landings would take place somewhere else and that our region would be spared as it had been, miraculously, in 1940. Providence decided otherwise".

On the German side, the commander-in-chief of the Western Armies was Marshal von Rundstedt, but he had little room for manoeuvre and was thus uneasy. Besides this, his second-in-command, Erwin Rommel, had direct links with the Führer. Von Rundstedt did not believe that the Atlantic Wall could defend the European shores efficiently: he considered it as a "gigantic bluff, less for the enemy which knows its possibilities thanks to their agents and other information sources, than for the German population". On September 29th 1942 the decision was taken to build, between then and the summer of 1943, 15 to 20 pillboxes per mile along the coastline. In July 1943, only 8 out of the planned 15,000 had been built. Considering that the aim could not be achieved, Hitler focused his efforts on the Pas-de-Calais: 517,000 obstacles, among them 31,000 mines, were set there.

On the other hand, Rommel thought that he could play a decisive role, if only he had significant reinforcements. In a matter of a few months he built 4,000 constructions and planted thousands of wooden posts on the beaches together with cement blocks and a variety of obstacles. The dunes were mined and the exits from the beaches closed by barbed wire networks or anti-tank walls.

Thousands of acres of fields and pastures were flooded and the "Rommel asparagus" was planted

Rommel in Normandy.

Marshal Erwin Rommel (1891-1944)

He joined the army in 1910 and was wounded three times during the First World War. He was promoted to General in 1939, and then to Marshal in 1942. In June 1940, he crossed Normandy with the 7th Panzer. Hero of the Wehrmacht and appreciated by Hitler, he became famous at the head of the Afrika Korps in Libya, when he was given the name of "The Desert Fox". At the end of 1943, he inspected the Atlantic defences and was named head

of the B group armies. On D-Day he returned to Germany, and then quickly came back to Normandy. He took part in the officers' plot against Hitler on July 20th. He was seriously wounded by an Allied plane at Sainte-Foy-de-Montgomery. The circumstances surrounding his death on October 14th 1944 remain obscure: according to some, he died from his wounds, while according to others Hitler forced him to commit suicide.

Czech hedgehog defences.

BUY THAT INVASION BOND!

against gliders. Despite these measures, the Germans seemed weakened because of their inferior air power: in spring 1944, only 500 planes were in flying condition. Von Rundstedt had to defend about 3,000 miles of coastline with roughly 700,000 men. But he did not have the best units, on average they were relatively old and there were many "Osttruppen", that is Soviet or Polish prisoners incorporated either willingly or unwillingly into the German army. In addition, Hitler remained convinced that an invasion could only take place in a port whereas the Allies had abandoned this possibility since their setback at Dieppe. Despite this situation, the morale of certain troops was high, such as the 12th SS Panzerdivision "Hitlerjugend". But the morale of many German soldiers, convinced that the war was already lost, was very low.

Finally, Rommel and von Rundstedt quarrelled over strategy: the former wanted to stop the Allied landings on the beaches while the latter thought it preferable to let the Allies land and then mount a powerful counter-offensive using armoured divisions to force them back into the sea. Opposed to von Rundstedt, Rommel asked for armoured reserves to be based near the shore. Hitler took the decision and only allotted him three Panzerdivisions. Rommel was aware that any attempt to land in France had to be quashed immediately, since the risk for Germany was so great. On April 22nd 1944 he told his aide-de-camp: *"Believe me, Lang, the first twenty-four hours will be decisive... The fate of Germany will depend on it... For the Allies and for us, this will be the longest day"*.

In order to succeed, the Allies spent months preparing a vast combined and mobilised operation to attack on June 5th, with 150,000 men, 20,000 vehicles, 11,000 planes and 7,000 ships. Every military action required follow-up logistics. It is one thing to establish a bridgehead, but to secure it is quite another. In the United States, Canada, Great Britain and the whole of the Commonwealth, everyone was ready to go and liberate Europe from the Nazi yoke. The many propaganda posters printed in the Allied countries are evidence of this.

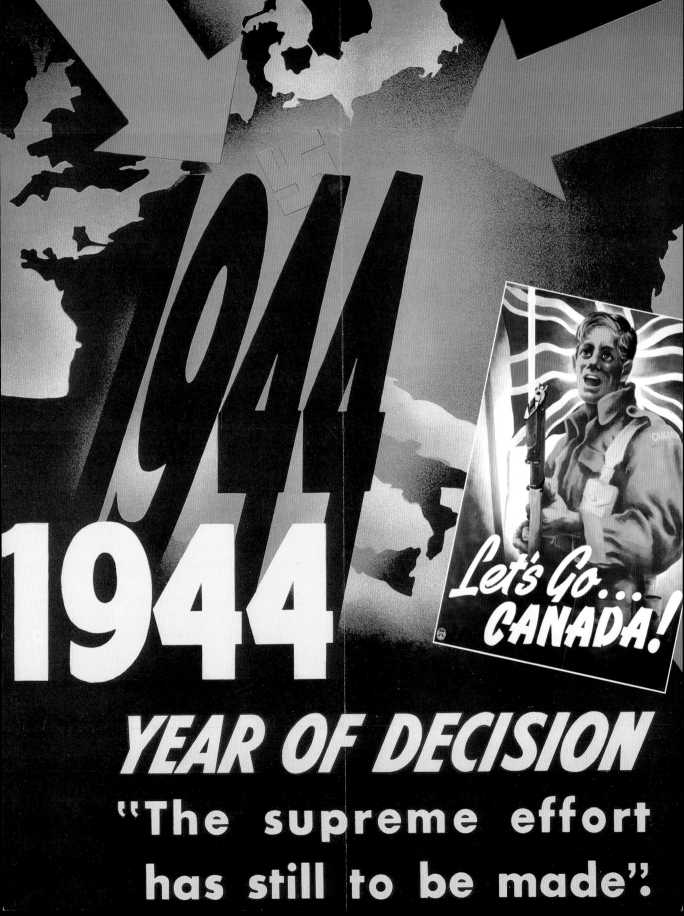

1944

YEAR OF DECISION

"The supreme effort has still to be made".

Let's Go...
CANADA!

The landings of June 6th 1944

Two weeks before D-Day, the soldiers of the assault divisions were sent to camouflaged camps situated near the boarding zones. For these soldiers, any further contact with the local population or with their families was now cut. On June 1st, men and equipment took their places aboard the ships.

The climax was approaching, and plunged the Allies into increasing anxiety. Whereas the month of May had been relatively pleasant, the first days of June were predicted to be more unsettled. The meteorological services noted that a depression was forming over Ireland and beginning to move south. On June 4th, the team of meteorologists led by Group Captain Stagg announced bad weather for the two following days with low cloud, a strong wind and rough seas: and these were the very days planned for the landings. The bad weather of June 5th made it especially difficult. So Eisenhower decided on a delay of at least twenty-four hours. This decision involved calling back the ships which were already getting under way. When the storm hit southern England, Eisenhower congratulated himself on his prudence, but he remained worried about the following day. Luckily, Group Captain Stagg's meteorologists announced that it would be calmer in the morning of June 6th, and that this weather could

last for thirty-six hours. The Supreme Commander of the Allied forces therefore decided at 4.15 a.m. to launch the attack at dawn on June 6th. All the ships converged on the Isle of Wight during the day of June 5th to be ready to cross the Channel. The assembly point was named "Piccadilly Circus".

Like the Normans, the Germans had been waiting for several months for a landing on the north-west shores of France. But the bad weather at the beginning of June convinced them that the Allied assault would be delayed for a certain time. Thus, on the morning of June 5th, Rommel left for Erlingen in Germany to see his family and to meet the Führer. At the same moment the generals of the VIIth German army went to Rennes for a meeting. During this time, the convoys were advancing across the Channel. The disembarkment landing craft (LCT, Landing Craft Tank) crossed slowly at 4 to 5 knots. In order to keep up the illusion that Operation Fortitude was still in action, RAF bombers dropped little metallic sheets called "windows" in the skies over the Pas-de-Calais and Caux.

In the evening of the 5th, Eisenhower had visited the "screaming eagles", the paratroopers of the 101st US airborne division. He said to one of them *"Good luck for tonight, soldier"*, knowing full well that the first

Canadian soldiers boarding.

Eisenhower talking to American paratroops a few hours before their boarding.

steps the Allied soldiers took on the Normandy beaches would be tragic.

Beginning at 9.00 p.m., the English radio began to churn out a series of messages aimed at the French Resistance to prepare the ground for Operation Overlord. *"The dice are on the mat"* and *"The long wails of the autumn violins wound my heart with a monotonous languor"* informed the resistants that D-Day was for the next day. The Germans knew the significance of the verses of Verlaine, but the information was not transmitted efficiently. On June 6th, Eisenhower addressed all the soldiers, aviators and sailors before they attacked the Normandy coasts: *"We can only accept total victory. Good luck to everyone and we*

implore the blessing of God Almighty for this great and noble enterprise". After midnight, the 6th British division under General Richard Gale launched its gliders to the northeast of Caen while the American paratroopers jumped over Sainte-Mère-Eglise: Overlord had begun. These parachute drops were at the two ends of the landings in order to protect the assault from the sea on the beaches.

Each army corps had its mission to operate in a well-defined geographical sector with a precise task. Thanks to the many aerial photographs and the information transmitted by the French resistants, the Allies were well acquainted with the terrain they were entering. Therefore, on June 6th, just after midnight, the British paratroops were the first to go into action north-east of Caen. Their mission was to take the Ranville and Bénouville bridges intact, at that time the only passing points over the river Orne and the canal linking Caen to the sea. The attack, rehearsed several times on an exact replica, was expertly led by Major Howard. One cannot say the same for the American para-troops dropped on Sainte-Mère-Eglise and scattered in the marshes in the middle of the département of the Manche: the swamps could not be detected by aerial photos. These first assaults backed up by general bomb-ing of all their positions shook the Germans who still could not believe in a large-scale landing. These bomb-ings destroyed 74 of the 92 German radar stations in Normandy. By applying the "violet" plan, the Nor-man resistants were able to mix up communications: for example, the telephone cable from Cherbourg to Rennes, passing through Saint-Lô, was cut at Pontaubault by members of the PTT (Post-Office) resistance network. Nonetheless information could pass, but not enough to con-vince the German general staff that D-Day had come. Besides this, after listening to Wagner's music on the evening of the 5th, Adolf Hitler went to sleep and there was no question of waking him up!

At dawn on Tuesday June 6th 1944, an immense armada of 7,000 ships of all types was closing in on the shores of the départements of Manche and Calvados. On board, more than 300,000 men who had crossed the Channel through furious seas, many of them seasick. But despite all this they were ready to land. For their part, planes and warships dropped thou-sands of tons of bombs on the Atlantic Wall. The weather that morning of the 6th of June was grey over the beaches of Calvados and Manche. As far as the Allied soldiers were concerned, they only knew them under five code names:

— **Sword Beach**, between Ouistreham and Lion-sur-Mer, assigned to the British 3rd division under General Rennie;

— **Juno Beach**, bet-ween Luc-sur-Mer and Graye-sur-Mer, assi-gned to the Canadian 3rd infantry division under General Keller;

— **Gold Beach**, between Graye-sur-Mer and Arro-manches-les-Bains, assigned to the Brit-ish 50th infantry division under General Graham;

— **Omaha Beach**, between Colleville-sur-Mer and Vierville-sur-Mer, assigned to the American 5th army corps of Gen-eral Gerow comprising the "Big Red One" of General Huebner;

— **Utah Beach**, on the eastern coast of the Cotentin peninsula, assigned to the American 7th army corps of General Collins comprising the American 4th infantry division of General Barton.

The Americans landed at 6.30 a.m. at Omaha and Utah while at 7.30 a.m. the Commonwealth troops reached the Sword, Juno and Gold beaches. At 6.30 a.m. Radio Berlin announced the lan-dings. In its morning edition, the title of the *New York Times* read "The Allies have landed in France". The great invasion was under way. General de Gaulle spoke on the BBC in the after-noon: "The final battle has begun". Hitler was informed at about 10 o'clock on June 6th that the landings were taking place on the Normandy beaches. He hardly seemed surprised but consi-dered that it was only a diversion and that a much more powerful attack would take place in the Pas-de-Calais. Therefore, he refused to move more than two armoured units to the west, the Panzer Lehr and the 12th SS Panzerdivision "Hitlerjugend".

Allied tract dropped by plane over Normandy on June 6th. On the back "General Eisenhower addresses the people of the occu-pied countries."

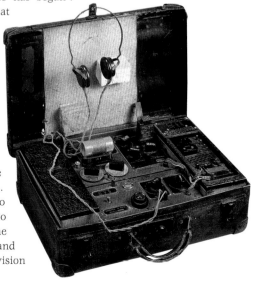

MK2 portable transmitter which the Resistance used to communi-cate with London.

Arromanches.

Utah Beach, June 6th 1944.

The landing operations continued throughout this day of June 6th, either without great difficulty as at Utah Beach, or with considerable loss of life as at Omaha Beach. By the evening, the Allied armies were well established on the coast of Lower Normandy. Most of the German defences and batteries had been neutralised. Over 150,000 men and 20,000 vehicles had landed. In only a few hours, the Allied soldiers managed to penetrate several miles inland. Not all the aims had been achieved, but the five landing beaches were well held. The counter-attack of the 21st Panzerdivision on the Périers ridge had been contained by the British. But the advance of the Allied armies turned out to be more difficult than expected, for example in Caen which had to be abandoned very quickly and was only fully liberated on July 19th, more than a month later. German resistance proved to be fiercer than expected, despite a relative absence of command. As Jean Compagnon emphasises *"they used the terrain well, fired accurately, reassembled quickly and resisted every inch of the way"*. The movement of the German reserves towards Normandy was delayed by the action of French resistants: thus the 2nd SS Panzerdivision "Das Reich", commanded by General Lammerding, put on alert in the evening of June 6th, only reached the south of Caen on June 28th! Even if Hitler demanded that *"each man must fight and die at his post"*, Rommel was much more pessimistic six days after the landings: *"The enemy is reinforced by the protection of greatly superior air power. Our aviation and our navy are incapable of providing adequate opposition. The enemy is reinforced much faster than our reserves arrive... Our position is extremely difficult: the foe prevents our making any movements during the day while itself it reorganises its own forces quite freely, even by air. The enemy has total control in the air over the combat zone and up to 60 miles inland".*

The days following June 6th saw an increasing number of bridgeheads being established, and by the evening of June 12th there were 16 Allied divisions present comprising more than 320,000 men accompanied by 54,000 vehicles and over 100,000 tons of equipment and supplies. This enabled the Allies to consolidate their positions in the following weeks before breaking through the German defences. The Allied superiority in the air was strengthened by building airstrips beginning on June 9th.

The battles for the liberation of Normandy, an essential prelude to the liberation of Europe, were to cost a high price both in loss of life and heavy destruction. Cities, towns and villages collapsed under the bombing. The Battle of Normandy ended in the Falaise-Chambois Pocket where the troops of the IIIrd Reich were surrounded and then defeated on August 21st 1944. This meant that the route to Paris and towards the east of France was now open, but it had taken two-and-a-half months instead of the estimated three weeks.

These days, the beaches of Calvados and Manche receive many tourists each year, but each of their steps

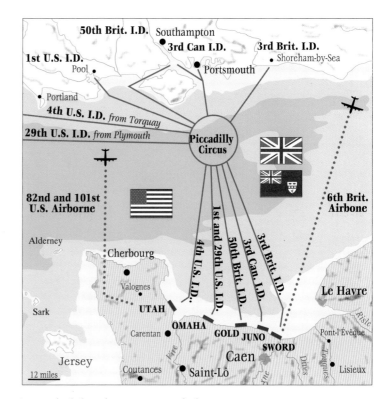

is marked by the memory of the biggest combined landing operation of all time. Each beach is a place of memory where those who pass by are asked to remember that thousands of men came here and died for the sake of freedom.

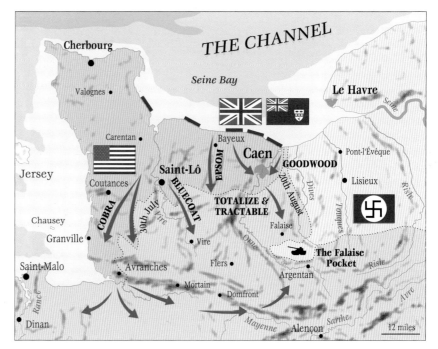

The British airborne sector

Twenty minutes after midnight, the British paratroops and commandos launched an attack on the sector located immediately to the east of the river Orne. They were carrying out the mission planned by General Richard Gale, commander of the 6th airborne division: *"Take and hold the bridges on the Caen canal and on the Orne at Bénouville and Ranville... It is important for future operations that the bridges be taken intact".* This assault was intended to allow the British 3rd infantry division landing at Sword Beach to reach Caen rapidly. The task of the 6th airborne division was to occupy the sector between the rivers Orne and Dives north of the Colombelles-Sannerville-Troarn road and to launch attacks in order to delay the movement of the German reserves advancing from the east and the south-east. The parachute drops were not all successful, and some were scattered in flooded marshland shrouded in damp fog. Eighty-four Canadian paratroopers were taken prisoner as a result.

Bénouville and Ranville

Twenty minutes after midnight Operation Tonga was launched: it was the first of a long series of operations within the framework of the Overlord plan. Three plywood Horsa gliders, which had been towed from England at 2,000 metres by Stirlings or Halifaxes, and each carrying 30 men from the 2nd Oxford light infantry battalion of Buckinghamshire integrated into the 6th Airborne, landed on the narrow strip of land separating the canal from the river Orne, less than 50 yards from the Bénouville swing-bridge. They made up the Airborne D company and were led by Major John Howard. In the lead glider, everyone was loudly singing the tunes sung several months before during training. At the moment they hit the ground at nearly 100 mph, the soldiers were holding each others' arms. The glider stopped only a few yards from the bridge. Willy Parr, a 22-year old English soldier remembers: *"The pilot*

General Richard Gale, commander of the British 6th airborne division.

Left page:
British soldiers at Pegasus Bridge.

Horsa gliders.

John Howard

John Howard joined the army in 1932 and was assigned to the airborne forces; he specialised in taking bridges and therefore was put in command of the attack on Bénouville bridge: he became part of the legend of Pegasus Bridge. Seriously hurt in a road accident in Great Britain in November 1944, he had to leave the army and ended up as a government employee.

AIRBORNE

Emblem of the 6th Airborne.

The Gondrée cafe, Bénouville.

British airborne troops in a glider.

landed about twenty yards from the bridge. It was incredible!" The Glider Pilots belonged to the army and had been trained specially for precision landings.

The two German guards were not aware of anything and were taken completely by surprise. The bridge was taken in ten minutes: this was the first victorious exploit of D-Day. Major Howard set up his headquarters in a little village cafe-dancing belonging to the Gondrée family.

Major Howard's men resisted all the German counter-attacks and held the bridge until the arrival of reinforcements, who were only two-and-a-half minutes late! These days this bridge is known as Pegasus Bridge in memory of the British airborne troops whose emblem was Pegasus.

At 1.30 p.m. on June 6th, commando No. 4 led by Lieutenant-Colonel Dawson, which had landed six hours earlier on Sword Beach, crossed the bridge to join Major Howard's men. Brigadier S. F. Lord Lovat, commander of the 1st special service brigade, was followed by his personal "piper" Bill Millin, playing "Blue bonnets over the border". At the same time the Ranville bridge was taken and resolutely defended, the paratroopers pushing back eight German counter-attacks. This conquest was announced as "ham and jam" by the BBC. In November 1993, Pegasus Bridge was dismantled and replaced by another better adapted to modern traffic conditions. A *son et lumière* is organised there every summer.

Taking these two bridges was the first Allied victory of the Battle of Normandy. Bénouville was quickly liberated, the first French town-hall of metropolitan France.

The village of Ranville was liberated at 2.30 a.m. by the 13th Lancashire paratrooper battalion. The British soldiers assembled around the old mill and attacked the German garrison in Ranville. This was the first village in metropolitan France to be liberated. An hour later, General Gale, after his trip on the Horsa No. 70 glider, set up his headquarters in lower Ranville: his statue can be seen today on June 6th Square. During the day of the 6th, the paratroopers had to push back two German counter-attacks. There is a cemetery next to the neo-gothic church where 2,151 British paratroopers and commandos are

Bénouville town-hall.

buried. Amongst them, Lieutenant Dan Brotheridge, the first to be killed in the Battle of Normandy at the approach to the Bénouville bridge.

1- *The original Pegasus Bridge.*
2- *The old bridge dismantled.*
3- *The Pegasus Bridge today.*
4- Son et lumière.

1 - Ranville military cemetery.
2 - Tomb of
Dan Brotheridge.
3 - German graves at Ranville.

Colonel Jean Piron (1896-1974)

After military school, he took part in the First World War, and ended as Captain. In 1940 he was named joint chief-of-staff of the Belgian 5th army corps. He was imprisoned by the Germans, and his escapes were stopped twice. However, the third time he succeeded and managed to reach England. In 1943, he took over the command of the Belgian 1st brigade and led it victoriously from Normandy to Brussels during the summer of 1944.

Plaque on the old mill of Ranville, in memory of the Piron Brigade.

There are also 323 German graves and 5 French graves in this cemetery.

Opposite, there is a plaque on the old mill in memory of the Belgian brigade commanded by Jean Piron.

Merville

These days, walking along the banks from Merville point to the mouth of the river Orne is very pleasant. Here, the sea goes out very far and opens up vast sandbanks. In the dunes there are still the remains of one of the three redoubts built in 1770 to defend the Orne estuary. South of the town, one-and-a-half miles from the shore, two blockhouses of a German battery defended by 130 soldiers still stands. Four concrete shelters hold four 100 mm guns with a 5 mile range. This battery, aimed at the Orne estuary, was considered to be the most important target in the region after the Bénouville and Ranville bridges. The battery was defen-

ded by anti-aircraft guns, by searchlights, and also included an observation bunker. Seven hundred and fifty paratroopers from the 9th battalion of the 6th airborne division commanded by Lieutenant-Colonel Terence B. N. Otway had had a tough training for more than two months. They were equipped with

the latest techniques. On June 6th, the paratroopers landed at about one o'clock in the morning, but only two gliders, including that of Otway, ended up in the right place; most of them were scattered around the battery. In an hour-and-a-half, Otway managed to

Merville pillbox.

assemble 150 men and decided to attack. At 4.45 a.m., after having lost half of his soldiers, Otway launched a rocket meaning "aim fulfilled". This was only half an hour before bombardments started up again from the *Arethusa* cruiser out at sea. Otway and his men found nothing but old Czech cannons. The German garrison was destroyed: out of 200 men, 178 were dead or unfit to fight. The spot was fought over repeatedly by the British and the Germans, and the battery changed hands seven times before August 17th. A battery museum has been set up on the site to emphasise the audacity and courage of Terence Otway and his paratroopers.

Surroundings

A certain number of Canadian paratroopers from the 8th battalion landed scattered in the Bavent woods. The German stronghold of Bréville controlled a crossroads from where they sent out counter-attacks against the points taken by the Allies. A memorial stone dedicated to the paratroopers of the 6th Airborne recalls the fierce fighting which preceded the liberation of the commune on June 13th. From the morning of June 6th, the bridges of Troarn, Bures-les-Monts and Robehomme on the river Dives were neutralised so as to cut road communications, in particular the Caen-Rouen road, but these communes were only liberated on August 17th.

The site of Merville.

At the same time, Canadian paratroopers destroyed the Varaville bridge on the Divette. Not far away, the Banneville-Sannerville cemetery holds the graves of 2,175 British soldiers.

Amfreville saw the link-up of the Kieffer commando and those of Lord Lovat on June 6th. At Hérouvillette there is a memorial to the 2nd Ox and Bucks, and 27 graves in the local cemetery are evidence of the violence of the battles at the moment of the first assault on June 7th. But the village was only liberated on July 18th during Operation Goodwood.

In the evening of June 6th, the 6th Airborne had managed to take control of the Bénouville and Ranville bridges and had neutralised the Merville battery. Twenty-two gliders had been lost, with men and equipment, but the other 74 had carried in 4,310 men. The last stage was Operation Mallard with the arrival of 216 Horsa gliders carrying men and supplies and 30 Hamilcar gliders carrying heavy equipment. They all landed north of Ranville near Saint-Aubin-d'Arquenay. The link-up with the troops of General Rennie who landed on Sword Beach was accomplished. However, they did not make enough progress to manage to take over the city of Caen in the evening of June 6th.

Bust of Lieutenant-Colonel Terence B. N. Otway at Merville.

Troarn memorial stone.

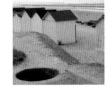

Sword Beach

The troops of the British 3rd infantry division landed on June 6th at 7.30 a.m. on the beaches of Colleville-sur-Orne, Lion-sur-Mer and Saint-Aubin-sur-Mer. The mission of General T. D. Rennie was to position his men on the right bank of the river Orne, to establish links with the 6th Airborne and the Canadian 3rd infantry division and to take Caen and Carpiquet airport by the evening of June 6th. This sector was defended by four long-range gun batteries: Merville, which was assigned to the British airborne troops, Riva-Bella, Ouistreham and Colleville-sur-Mer. In order to defend this sector, the German general staff had the 716th infantry division and above all the 21st Panzerdivision stationed to the south of Caen. But it could also call on the 12th SS Panzerdivision "Hitlerjugend" based near Evreux. Under the command of Kurt Meyer, this was composed entirely of young Nazi fanatics aged between 17 and 20 years old.

Colleville-Montgomery

The Morris stronghold, installed in several houses camouflaged behind a hedge, was defended by four 105 mm cannons in pillboxes. When the attack was launched by the men of the First Suffolk Regiment, at about 1 o'clock in the afternoon, the Germans came out carrying a white flag and surrendered. Colleville's main defence was the Hillman site, a concrete ensemble about 600 yards long sheltering the headquarters of the 736th grenadiers regiment, and protected by minefields, networks of barbed wire and machine guns. The First Suffolk had to make two assaults before they took this stronghold at about 8 o'clock in the evening. The Hillman site, comprising twelve half-buried concrete ensembles linked together by underground passages and spread over an area of 50 acres, is cared for by a local association.

Landing on Sword Beach.

Left page:
Landing at Hermanville.

Remains of German defences at Colleville-Montgomery.

Memorial stone at Colleville.

The commune of Colleville-sur-Orne is now called Colleville-Montgomery in memory of Field Marshal Montgomery, commander of the 21st army group.

The beach was taken as early as June 6th. There is a memorial stone made by Patrick Heleyne in 1994, facing a block-house, in memory of the Allied liberators.

Blockhouse at Colleville-Montgomery.

View of the beach.

Ouistreham-Riva-Bella

At 7.20 a.m. naval artillery opened fire on Ouistreham and Riva-Bella to prepare the way for the soldiers who were about to land. The battery equipped with 155 mm cannons defending the Riva-Bella beach had been moved in May 1944 on the orders of Rommel and reinstalled in the woods of Saint-Aubin-d'Arquenay. To the east of the mouth of the river Orne, the vast Riva-Bella beach was defended by a long concreted ditch. On June 6th at 8.30 a.m. 177 French troops from the 1st battalion of the Royal marines of the 4th Franco-British commando, led by Lieutenant-Commander Philippe Kieffer, landed here. Most of them, mainly Bretons, had rejoined de Gaulle in 1940. They had trained hard in Scotland, at Achnacarry camp. This was the only French unit involved on D-Day. They were integrated into the 1st brigade commanded by Lord Lovat. Thirty were put out of action almost immediately after the landing. The others continued towards Riva-Bella by the Lion-sur-Mer road so as to take the enemy from behind. The aim was to capture the casino which had been transformed into a small fort by the German defence. The old casino in the Anglo-Normand style was demolished in 1942 to be rebuilt as a stronghold with two 20 mm guns on the roof. A veteran of the 1914-18 war, from Ouistreham, guided the green berets across town so that they could take the casino from the rear. However, tanks had to be brought into action for the mission to succeed.

A villa, located these days behind the monument to commando No. 4, served as rallying point for the commandos and as a forward medical post. Access to this beach was defended by fortifications equipped with a battery of six 155 mm cannons, machine guns and mines: nearly half the green berets perished here. A steel dome sheltering the machine guns overlooks the beach.

Slightly apart from the coast road stands the Grand Bunker; a con-

crete tower 55 feet high. This building has five floors, and the highest has a wide slit for observation and

Remains of German defences on the Ouistreham-Riva-Bella beach.

Philippe Kieffer (1890-1962)

This marine-commander, an escapee from Dunkirk, joined General de Gaulle in London in 1940. First of all he was assigned to the battleship Courbet *and then, in 1942, he joined the British commandos. With several Frenchmen he formed the 1st battalion of the Royal marines under the command of Lord Lovat. He took part in Operation Jubilee against Dieppe in August 1942. His commando was the only French unit to land on June 6th.*

He wrote: "At this precise moment, the earth and the sea seemed lifted up in a crash of thunder: mortar bombs, the whistling of artillery shells, the terrible yapping of machine guns; everything seemed concentrated on us." Later he tried to enter politics in Calvados: he was elected general counsellor of Isigny in 1945, but was beaten in the general elections of 1946.

Memorial stone to Philippe Kieffer at Ouistreham.

The flame monument at Ouistreham.

for setting up a telemeter for adjusting the range of fire. An Atlantic Wall museum is to be found here now: on the 5th floor, it is possible to look at the horizon through the telemeter and to see as far as 28 miles on an arc of 180°. Not far from here, another museum, the Commando No. 4 museum, recounts the action of the green berets under Philippe Kieffer. Near the embarkation port for England one finds a lighthouse monument. Ouistreham was liberated at 1 o'clock in the afternoon, but only 60 French commandos were still fit to fight. A monument in the shape of a flame, on Boulevard Aristide-Briand, recalls the sacrifice of the Free French on June 6th 1944. This work in aluminium, on top of a dome, is by Yvonne Guégan, an artist from Caen.

Near it, a memorial stone pays tribute to Philippe Kieffer.

The XIth and XIIth century Norman church has a stained glass window offered by the Commando Association in honour of the action of the marine commandos on D-Day. The picture is by the painter Raymond Bradley; at the base is the inscription: "1939-1945. To the glory of God".

Hermanville-sur-Mer

The landing took place in the narrow sector between the Hermanville breach and Lion-sur-Mer. Despite the swell of the tide, the British managed to disembark 21 of their 25 amphibious tanks. The commune was liberated around 10 o'clock in the morning by the South Lancashire Regiment. At sea, at just over a mile from this breach, flying the flag of the Free French, the cross of Lorraine, the *Gustave-Courbet* battleship was scuttled to act as a "blockship", thus forming a breakwater with six cargoes and two other warships. The coast road is now named after Admiral Wietzel, the last captain of the *Gustave-Courbet;* the admiral laid his battleship flag in the town-hall. The chapel has stained-glass windows commemorating the landing. Near an XVIIIth century manor, there is a cemetery of 986 graves of British and French commandos.

On the village square, the visitor can see the well of the Saint-Pierre pond, cited by the British army for supplying 7 million litres of water between June 6th at 7 o'clock in the evening until July 1st. Thirty taps are to be seen along the wall of the Presbytère. In the neighbouring woods, the British set up twelve field hospitals.

Opposite:
The Courbet *scuttled.*

The Saint-Pierre well, at Hermanville-sur-Mer.

Landing at Hermanville-sur-Mer, June 6th 1944.

Lion-sur-Mer

While he was inspecting the Atlantic Wall, Marshal Rommel was photographed in the company of his offi-cers at the end of the Rue des Bains in front of a half-timbered villa. This commune was liberated on June 7th by the 41st Royal Marines Commando after fierce fighting and the Haut-Lion castle was taken after two hours' resistance. There is a monument next to a tank in memory of the action of the British soldiers.

Luc-sur-Mer

At low tide the sea uncovers a beach of sand and pebbles where one can collect great quantities of seaweed. The beach is edged by a long promenade and a cliff pitted with notches eroded by the sea which are called "confessionals". This beach had been visited by a British commando on September 28th 1941: the aim of this raid was to take sand samples and to analyse them. There is a memorial stone in memory of this action with an invitation to the visitor: "Passer-by, stop and meditate". This memorial stone also commemorates the arrival of Lord Lovat's commandos and the 4th Special Service Brigade of Brigadier Leicester. Luc-sur-Mer was liberated on June 7th after a short encounter in the Petit-Enfer led by the 46th Royal Marine Commando.

However, the British troops did not advance fast enough, which enabled General Wilhelm Richter, commander of the 716th division of the German infantry, to move his defences north of Caen, into the Lébisey woods. This installation prevented Caen to be taken in the evening of June 6th, as planned by Operation Overlord. However, General Rennie managed to link up with the elements of the 6th Airborne Division which arrived early on June 6th on the other bank of the river Orne.

Monument to the 41st RMC at Lion-sur-Mer.

Stèle à Luc-sur-mer.

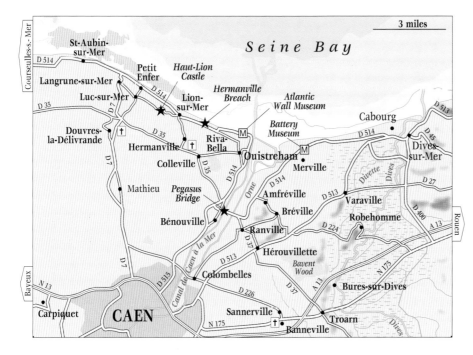

J u n o   B e a c h

The Canadian 3rd infantry division under Major General R. F. L. Keller, comprising 15,000 Canadians and 9,000 British troops, set foot on the beaches of Vaux at Saint-Aubin-sur-Mer on June 6th just before 8 o'clock in the morning; heavy seas having delayed them by twenty minutes. The mission was to advance on Caen and take its airport, Carpiquet. These Canadian soldiers wanted their revenge after Dieppe, but the beaches of this sector were defended by pillboxes sheltering cannons and machine guns. About 14,000 mines had been set as well as other obstacles of all kinds. Nonetheless, the German defensive system was not very powerful on this part of the shore. In fact, the Kriegsmarine specialists had decided that the rocks of Calvados should prevent any landing there. On June 6th, the leading Montreal daily newspaper, *La Presse*, saluted this Canadian landing with a front page title *"The Canadians see Normandy again"*.

Troops ready to land.

Left page:
Landing at Bernières,
June 6th 1944.

Major General Keller
at Bernières-sur-Mer.

Battery at Saint-Aubin-sur-Mer.

Langrune-sur-Mer

This town is known for its fine sandy beach bordered by a promenade, and has a XIIIth century church with a lantern tower topped by an elegant spire with pinnacle turrets. Most of the villas overlooking the sea-front were fortified by the Germans. A group of houses was transformed into a stronghold and equipped with 50 mm anti-tank cannons. The defences resisted during the whole of June 6th despite naval bombardments and fire from two light Centaur tanks. The commune was liberated on June 7th at about 3.30 p.m. after fierce fighting, the soldiers of the No. 48 commando led by Lieutenant-Colonel Moulton having to fight house by house, opening breaches in the garden walls. Commando No. 48 lost half its men here. The local cemetery shelters the cinders of two Allied soldiers. A memorial stone dedicated to the 48th Royal Marine Commando stands in a square along the sea wall.

Saint-Aubin-sur-Mer

During the night of August 3rd to 4th 1940 Maurice Duclos, called Saint-Jacques, returned to his commune, sent by General de Gaulle to estimate the German forces present and their installations. As at Luc-sur-Mer, this beach had been visited by a British commando making a reconnaissance raid during the night of September 27th to 28th 1941. Less than three years later, the Canadian soldiers landed there. The North Shore regiment encountered many problems, losing men and tanks on the beach because of German defences with a 50 mm cannon plus a large number of machine guns. After clearing the beach, the 22 amphibious tanks of the Garry Horse Fort came up against a pillbox. The 48th Royal Marine Commando landed during the second wave with the task of taking Langrune-sur-Mer. The soldiers killed on the Saint-Aubin beach are buried in the garden of a house near the sea wall. As for the school, it was used as a hospital. On the sea wall, just next to Bernières-sur-Mer, the Cassine battery remains. This stronghold was built on the grounds of a villa called La Cassine which the Germans knocked down to install several pillboxes linked by underground or open passages.

Near the battery one can still see a cannon next to the monument dedicated to the 48th Commando, together with a list of civilian and military victims.

Monument to the 48th RMC at Saint-Aubin-sur-Mer.

Bernières-sur-Mer

The beach is 1.5 miles long, and the Canadians of the Queen's Own Rifles and the Chaudière Regiment landed here. The beach looked like a forest of stakes since there were so many obstacles of all sorts. At 4 a.m., the Bernières beach was heavily bombed. However, this commune is situated in a sector where they live well, as an old Norman saying goes: "If you want to be happy, go and live between Caen and Bayeux". When the landing craft arrived at Bernières around 8.10 a.m., the Canadians had only about 100 yards between them and the beach. They landed under a hail of artillery shells. Ninety ships were destroyed, many beaching on the Bernières islands. The inhabitants of this commune were surprised when they were liberated on June 6th at 9.30 a.m. to hear the "Tommies" speaking French or singing "I have come back to see my Normandy", since many of them were youngsters from Quebec of Norman origin who joined up to liberate the Old Continent. Several confirmed their French origin by shouting: *"I'm not English but French Canadian"*. At 11.45. a.m. Major General Keller set up his command post in the Hotel de la Plage. And it is from there that the first reports for the

world agencies and newspapers were written.

As soon as it was liberated, the Bernières beach quickly piled up with tanks, trucks, caterpillars and cannons.

Douvres-la-Délivrande

Near this commune, famous for its Notre-Dame basilica and its annual fete in honour of the Black Virgin, on the road to Basly, was a German radar station with code-name "Distelfink" (Goldfinch). About a mile from the sea, this post could survey any naval operations coming from Britain. The ensemble comprised two Freya-type radars, one of the Wassermann type with a range of 190 miles and two of the Würzburg type. The post was protected by anti-aircraft defences and anti-tank cannons and had a telephone exchange, a radio station, an electric generator and an ammunition bay. But on June 6th, the Allies managed their jamming so well

Remembrance monument at Bernières-sur-Mer.

Bernières-sur-Mer, D-Day.

"Würzburg" radar.

Radar museum at Douvres-la-Délivrande.

phy explains the work of air or sea equipment. Outside one can see a "Würzburg Riese" radar. After having been recuperated by the British in 1944, three radars were assigned to the French Navy, then given to a physics laboratory. In 1957, two were transformed into radio-telescopes for the Nançay station. The museum site shows one of these pieces of equipment, one left over from 1,500 built by the Germans after August 1941.

Douvres-la-Délivrande, liberated on June 6th, served as the headquarters of the Canadian Major General George Francoeur. The Vierge-Fidèle monastery was turned into a hospital. At the entrance to Douvres, coming from Caen, one finds a British cemetery with 1,123 graves of combatants killed on the Sword and Juno beaches.

Bény-Reviers

On the road from Bernières to Bény, the Fief Pelloquin, a castle inhabited by the Hettier de Boislambert family, one of whose members had joined General de Gaulle in 1940, became the first Anglo-Canadian field hospital. Even though Bény-sur-

that even the last Würzburg radar which had withstood all the bombing from the air did not see the naval armada arriving. However, the station stood up to Allied attacks for eleven days. The garrison of 238 men surrendered on June 17th after gas was injected into the ventilation holes of the bunkers: the information had been provided by the French who had taken part in the building.

Today, the site serves as the first Radar museum. It demonstrates the role of radars and their technological development. A clear scenogra-

Canadian cemetery at Bény-Reviers.

Mer was well defended by the Mouli-neaux battery comprising four 100 mm cannons and located in the commune of Fontaine-Henri, it was liberated by the La Chaudière regiment on June 6th and an airstrip was built there. The Moulineaux battery was bombarded before 6 o'clock in the morning by the cruisers *Belfast* and *Diadem*. Between the communes of Bény-sur-Mer and Reviers there is a Canadian cemetery of 15 acres with 2,043 graves.

The neighbouring communes of Anguerny and Tailleville were also liberated on June 6th by Canadian soldiers. The telephone exchange set up in the castle was taken by the Canadian 8th brigade. The castle later became a leave centre for the Canadian soldiers.

Courseulles-sur-Mer

This little fishing port known for its oysters saw several Canadian units land on June 6th, in particular the First Hussars, the Regina Rifles, the Royal Winnipeg Rifles and the 1st Canadian Scottish.

The landing there was especially difficult. The regiment of Centaur tanks lost 34 out of 40. Held down under heavy fire from two pillboxes, one company lost two thirds of its men. The fierce fighting of the Regina Rifles, which had to advance house by house and street by street, liberated the commune about 10 a.m. At 8.30 a.m. the tank of sergeant Léo Gariépy of the First Hussars had attacked the Kommandantur. On the right bank of the estuary of the Seulles a Sherman DD (Duplex Drive) tank stands on a base; a vehicle weighing 32 tons which was sunk on June 6th and has been placed there in memory of the landing of the Canadian 2nd armoured division and dedicated to Léo Gariépy. Further on, on the banks of the Seulles, there is a German gun complete with cannon and set in its concrete housing.

From June 8th, the mouth of the river Seulles gave shelter to the first Allied supply port before the artificial

Canadian soldiers and tanks at Courseulles-sur-Mer.

Sherman DD tank at Courseulles-sur-Mer.

*Cross of Lorraine
at nightfall.*

port of Arromanches had been completed: 2,000 tons of supplies were disembarked each day. Twelve ships were sunk in order to form an artificial roadstead.

To the east of the jetty there is now a huge sword made out of teak; a monument dedicated to the Royal Winnipeg Rifles.

Graye-sur-Mer

The Royal Winnipeg Rifles, whose soldiers were nicknamed the "black devils", quickly took Graye-sur-Mer around 9 o'clock. But the sanatorium, defended by several Russian artillerymen, held out until the following day. Between Courseulles and Graye, General de Gaulle arrived on June 14th 1944 aboard the destroyer *La Combattante* to set foot on French soil again, accompanied among others by Generals Béthouart and Kœnig, and Maurice Schumann. The flag with the Cross of Lorraine from *La Combattante* has been kept in Courseulles. A monument in the form of the Cross of Lorraine recalls this moment.

Arrival of de Gaulle on French soil on June 14th 1944.

Blockhouse and signal-memorial at Graye-sur-Mer.

General de Gaulle left the Graye breach by Jeep to go to Creullet castle to meet Montgomery, who had landed here several days earlier. Several pill-boxes still remain on this beach, which was also chosen by Winston Churchill and King George VIth who disembarked here on June 12th and June 16th respectively.

At the exit from the beach, at the foot of the Cross of Lorraine, stands an AVRE-Churchill tank called "One Charlie" from the 79th armoured division, which was recovered in November 1976.

On June 6th at about 5 p.m. an operating theatre was set up in the kit-

"One Charlie" tank at Graye-sur-Mer.

chen of the Sainte-Thérèse holiday camp, to care for the wounded whose numbers were growing by the hour. On July 4th, the hospital was transferred to the sanatorium: at the beginning of the battle of Falaise this hospital received 2,700 wounded in a single day.

Creully

The Canadian soldiers advanced quickly inland, liberating the villages of Tierceville, Colombiers-sur-Seulles, Sainte-Croix-sur-Mer, Banville, Villons-les-Buissons and Le Fresne-Camilly on their way, before reaching Creully. General Montgomery set up his first headquarters at Sainte-Croix-sur-Mer before transferring it, the same day, to Creullet castle, which was lower down. Creully was liberated on June 17th at about 5.30 p.m. and served as a link-up point for the Canadian and British armies coming from the Gold and Juno sectors.

The castle, built between the XIIth and XVIth centuries, had already been occupied by the English in 1417. In 1944, the BBC installed a studio there for direct transmissions to London. On the door of the XIIth century tower hung a notice "BBC, silence please. No entry". The transmitter on the top of the tower worked every day in the months of June and July. Thus the journalist Chester Wilmot could cover the Battle of Normandy for the BBC. During the visit of the castle one can see an exhibition of equipment plus photographs taken by English, Canadian and French journalists.

From the terrace, one can see Creullet castle. In the park, between June 7th and 22nd, Montgomery installed his mobile headquarters camouflaged by stacks of hay. In the great salon of the castle, he received General de Gaulle, King George VIth and Winston Churchill.

The Canadian soldiers had completed their task of settling in on the Calvados coast by taking a supply port, Courseulles-sur-Mer. Twenty-four thousand men were disembarked with 2,000 vehicles. Losses were less than a thousand. Apart from setting up this solid beachhead they had advanced inland as far as Creuilly where they linked up with their British comrades who had landed on Gold Beach. But their advance to the east, that is towards Caen, was to be stopped for a month at the airfield of Carpiquet.

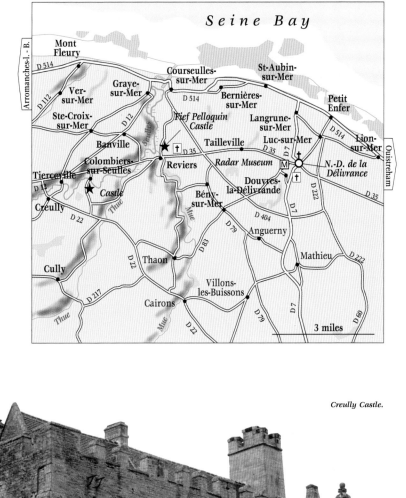

Creully Castle.

Gold Beach

At 7. 05 a.m., on the 3 miles of beaches between Ver-sur-Mer and Asnelles, 25,000 men landed from the 50th Northumbrian infantry division, accompanied by the 8th armoured division. The Northumbrian had proved itself during the French Campaign in May 1940, and then again in 1942 at El Alamein and in 1943 in Sicily. Among their motivations was revenge for the retreat from Dunkirk in 1940. General D. A. H. Graham was assigned the task of installing himself on the cliffs overlooking Arromanches and quickly taking the town of Bayeux. General Graham told his soldiers: "*All of you, officers and men of the 50th infantry division, have the honour of having been chosen to strike this formidable blow for freedom*". In the Gold sector, the British used "funnies": tanks with chain whips in front which could blow up the mines on the beaches, while others could destroy the pillboxes or were equipped with an anti-sinking system. The tank-dozer removed the obstacles placed on the beach whereas the "crocodile" was the most frightening with its flame-thrower. The landings were a great shock for the locals: as an inhabitant of Arromanches, Mlle Lenglet, wrote in her diary: "*Nothing has changed in Arromanches, but from Saint-Côme and Courseulles one only sees ships, a wonderful and unforgettable sight which compensates for our previous hours*".

Ver-sur-Mer

The landing took place at 7. 25 a.m. in the Rivière hamlet without any great problems, so much so that an hour later, the British troops had advanced half a mile inland and the site was cleaned in the following hours. The 5th East Yorkshire fusiliers then went on to the Mont Fleury battery 1/2 mile away. The commune of Ver-sur-Mer, decorated in 1948 by the Military Cross, has paid homage to the 2nd Hertfordshire battalion. The America Gold Beach Museum shows the victorious assault of the 69th Northumbrian brigade in the King sector. It is in memory of all the soldiers who landed at Ver-sur-Mer and who liberated Bayeux. In the town is a house where Admiral Ramsay installed his headquarters. From above or from the coastal road leaving the village, one can see the high Arromanches cliffs.

Left page:
Landing at Ver-sur-Mer.

On the Ver-sur-Mer promenade today.

*Remains of the
Mont Fleury battery.*

Tomb of Maurice Schumann.

Maurice Schumann (1911-1998)

*A journalist, he joined de Gaulle in 1940. In July 1944, he made a daily broadcast in French on the BBC: he became the spokesman of the Free French.
After landing at Asnelles, he arrived at Bayeux for the liberation of the town.
Later, with the FFI (French Forces of the Interior) he took part in the liberation of the right bank of Caen.
Companion of the Liberation, he entered politics after the war at the side of General de Gaulle. He was elected member of parliament, then senator; he was Minister of Foreign Affairs from 1969 to 1971. In 1974, he became a member of the Académie française.*

Asnelles blockhouse.

To the west of Ver-sur-Mer, under Mont Fleury castle, there was a battery of the same name, with four Russian cannons of 122 mm, two in pillboxes and two in the open. The range of this battery was 9 miles. To the south-east was the Mare Fontaine battery equipped with four Czech 105 mm cannons installed in cube-shaped pillboxes. These two batteries, which could cover the whole of Gold Beach with their fire, were destroyed by bombing from the air and by fire from the cruisers *Orion* and *Belfast*, and mopping up operations were carried out in the morning of June 6th by soldiers of the 6th and 7th Green Howards. Sergeant-major Stan Hollis was given the only Victoria Cross awarded on D-Day. This soldier showed great bravery by capturing two blockhouses and by saving the lives of two soldiers under enemy fire. At Mont Fleury there still exist two pillboxes invaded by vegetation.

Asnelles-sur-Mer

The 1st Hampshire Regiment of the 231st brigade landed on this beach, but throughout the whole of June 6th it met fierce opposition from the German defences installed in small fortifications in Hamel. The rest of the 231st brigade landed further east and met with less resistance, since the Russian soldiers were little motivated and fled as soon as the firing started. Thanks to their "funnies", the British soldiers cleared the terrain, reached Meuvaines and occupied the strongholds overlooking Arromanches. The coast road crosses the village of Meuvaines, where the German artillery command post for shore defences was installed. An airstrip was set up there. Since 1998, at the far end of the new little cemetery, is the isolated tomb of Maurice Schumann, spokesman for the Free French.

Saint-Côme-de-Fresné

Before arriving in Arromanches-les-Bains, there is a panoramic table on the cliff with an excellent viewpoint over the Gold Beaches to the east and the remains of the artificial harbour. This is the emplacement of a former German radar station surrounded by concrete bunkers holding anti-aircraft defences (DCA). This radar station was installed on the Arromanches cliffs together with a Freya-type long-range detection equipment, a Würzburg-type radar and two others which were more powerful: a Mammut and a Wassermann. Their range could go up to 50 miles, but these radars were destroyed by the bombings several days before June 6th. After a few hours of fighting, Saint-Côme-de-Fresné was liberated in the afternoon. The panoramic table gives a clear idea of the location of the artificial harbour of Arromanches by showing where the ships were anchored.

Close to the panoramic table there is a statue of Notre-Dame-des-Flots. It was knocked off its pedestal by the Germans so that it could no longer serve as a reference point, and was re-erected after the war looking towards Arromanches, doubtless to thank Notre-Dame-des-Flots for her protection during the landings.

There still remain German pillboxes on the Saint-Côme-de-Fresné cliff.

When one leaves this commune one finds the shore artillery command post operating from Caen to Grand camp-les-Bains.

Pillbox at Saint-Côme-de-Fresné.

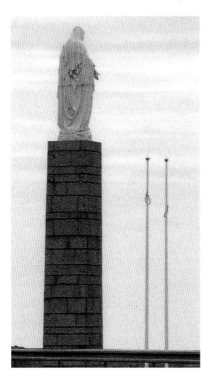

Notre-Dame-des-Flots.

Panoramic table at Saint-Côme-de-Fresné.

Arromanches-les-Bains

In order to defend this small tourist fishing port, the Germans built a pillbox on the cliff overlooking Arromanches and

for the landing troops while awaiting the taking of a major French port. Since the failure of the Dieppe expedition, there was no longer any question of taking over a harbour as such. Thus the idea to create one.

The two artificial ports, Mulberry A and B, were prefabricated in England and towed into place at 5 mph. They were at that time and still remain a technological challenge. On June 7th, the Arromanches artificial port or Mulberry B, called "Port Winston" after Winston Churchill whose idea it was, began to be put into place. To begin with, seventeen ships were sunk at sea to form a break-water of blockships called Gooseberry. Next, 115 "Phoenix" blocks representing 500,000 tons of concrete (each block being 200 ft long, 60 ft high and 50 ft wide and weighing 6,044 tons) plus a dozen pontoons or jetty heads were arranged so as to compose a huge artificial roadstead comprising 10 miles of routes. Mulberry A located at Vierville was for the American troops whereas Mulberry B was intended for the British troops. But the storm of June 19th to 22nd destroyed the Vierville artificial harbour, so much so that the supply operations had to be regrouped in Arromanches. The

Aerial view of the artificial port.

another on the Tracy-sur-Mer cliff.

Liberated at 6 p.m. by land, by tanks arriving from Saint-Côme-de-Fresne, this small town, together with its neighbour Vierville, was chosen by the Allies for the creation of two artificial disembarkment ports intended to provide supplies

Evacuation of wounded from Arromanches.

assembly time took almost a fortnight. At the same time, routes were traced out and the beaches cleared. Once this was finished, the ensemble as a whole represented a roadstead over 9 miles long able to harbour the biggest ships. On June 12th, that is only six days after the landings, over 300,000 men, 54,000 vehicles and 104,000 tons of supplies had been disembarked. This harbour quickly became more efficient than Cherbourg or Le Havre: during the 100 days it was used it disembarked 2.5 million men, 500,000 vehicles and 4 million tons of equipment and supplies. The port was protected from a possible German air attack by 150 anti-aircraft guns and by permanent barrage balloons.

These days, there are still several pontoons to be seen from all points of the coast.

The D-Day Landings Museum, inaugurated on June 5th 1954 by the President of the French Republic, René Coty, situated facing the remains of the artificial harbour, explains the building and operation of artificial

The D-Day Landings Museum at Arromanches.

ports by a working model of Port Winston together with a film. It also shows the different phases of the liberation of Normandy. Each Allied nation has a display window.

Arromanches 360, the third Circorama in France, shows an eighteen-minute film "The Price of Freedom" on nine screens in a round theatre. This film mixes archive footage and present-day pictures, plunging the spectator into the thick of the action.

Arromanches and the remains of the artificial harbour.

Sea view.

Longues-sur-Mer

This spot offers a superb range of vision over the sea from an altitude of 215 feet and was naturally chosen by the Germans in September 1943 to install a battery of four 150 mm cannons with a range of up to 12.5 miles. In front of this battery, 300 yards away, on the edge of the cliff, was observation post No. 83.

This battery was one of the dozen on the Normandy coast to open fire on the British fleet. The battery was heavily bombarded on May 28th and June 3rd, but without any destructive effect. Despite another intense pounding by 124 planes of the Royal Air Force, dropping 600 tons of bombs in the night of June 5th to 6th, the Longues battery resisted and opened fire at 5.37 a.m. on two American warships including the battleship *Arkansas*. Its firing range covered the two Allied sectors of Gold and Omaha Beach, which made this battery especially dangerous for the landings. The

decisive attack came from the sea, since the positions of the battery were known from information from the Resistance. The warships *Georges-Leygues, Montcalm, Ajax* and *Arkansas* took turns to fire on the battery and managed to destroy three-quarters of the cannons. The battery was put out of action com-

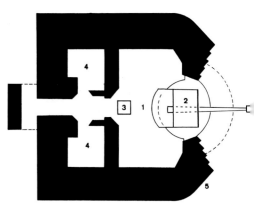

PLAN OF A PILLBOX
1. Firing chamber
2. Cannon
3. Ditch
4. Ammunition depot
5. Pier

pletely just before 7.00 p.m. by two shots from the *Georges-Leygues* battleship and occupied the following morning after the garrison surrendered.

The road leading to the cliff, tarred by the Germans, gives a view of the whole of the battery: three of the four pillboxes have been preserved with their artillery. Each pillbox measures 15 yards by ten. The roof slab and the walls are 6 feet thick,

Pillbox, Longues-sur-Mer.

which protected the guns aimed at the sea.

The pillboxes were half-hidden by a thick layer of earth. The ensemble was protected by machine guns, mines and layers of barbed wire. This is the only Atlantic Wall battery kept in this state with its cannons in their firing chamber. Above the cannons, one can see big conduits which are the remains of a ventilation system intended to extract poisonous gases produced by the firing.

The ensemble, which remains the best example of what was a naval artillery battery, now belongs to the Coast Conservatory and is protected by the Historic Monuments list.

After Longues-sur-Mer, the coast road leads to Le Chaos. One can also take the cliff path starting from the Vauban tower at Port-en-Bessin. Here one can see a well-preserved system of German defences as well as a firing direction post located ahead of the battery 300 yds from the edge of the cliff, complete with a telemeter to control the firing range.

Opposite: **View of the Longues-sur-Mer site.**

Le Chaos at Longues-sur-Mer.

Pillbox with cannon.

Remains of a pillbox overlooking Port-en-Bessin.

Port-en-Bessin

Overlooking the fishing port, beyond the Vauban tower, on the top of the 215 ft cliff there was an ensemble of German defences.

The town was liberated on June 8th by the 47th Royal Marine Commando after more than a day's resistance by the Germans and then, after June 14th, became a supply port: 1,000 tons of equipment and supplies were unloaded every day.

General view of Port-en-Bessin.

On June 25th it became the first land-based point for PLUTO - Pipe Line Under the Ocean - supplied by cargo ships anchored out at sea. By the end of August, 175,000 tons of fuel had been delivered, with daily highs of 8,000 tons. This pipeline, named "Minor system", was linked up to that from Sainte-Honorine-des-Pertes and connected at Saint-Lô to the "Major system" coming from the port of Cherbourg.

There is a plaque dedicated to the 47th Royal Marine Commando on the blockhouse beneath the Vauban tower.

At the entrance to Port-en-Bessin, in the village of Commes, one finds a museum of underwater wrecks. Twenty-five years of research on the sea bed enabled Jacques Lemonchois to raise hundreds of wrecks and a range of equipment and personal objects from inside the ships sunk during the landings, from bells from the destroyers *Isis* and *Swift* to tubes of toothpaste.

Port-en-Bessin marked the end of the British sector and the beginning of the American sector, especially that of Omaha which was so deadly.

Plaque to honour the 47th RMC and Vauban tower at Port-en-Bessin.

Commemorative monument on the beach.

Bayeux

This town, 10 miles inland, is the only one in Normandy to have been completely undamaged, since it was liberated by British troops at 10 a.m. on June 7th. On June 12th, General Eisenhower visited the town with his son, who was on leave. At the end of the dual carriageway coming from Caen there is a roundabout paying homage to Overlord's Supreme Commander. A huge statue seems to welcome visitors.

Two days after that, on June 14th, General de Gaulle arrived. Over two thousand people, happy to be liberated after four years of occupation, cheered him. He had come to set up the government of Free France with the nomination of the first government representative François Coulet

Dwight David Eisenhower (1890-1969)

His nickname was Ike. He was second to Mac Arthur at the beginning of the war, and then named commander-in-chief of the Allied armies in North Africa in November 1942. He went from success to success, in Tunisia, Sicily and Italy. After the Teheran conference, he was promoted to commander-in-chief of the Allied armies in Europe, in December 1943. His qualities as an organiser and diplomat were appreciated. On June 5th, he sent this message to the Allied soldiers: "The eyes of the world are upon you, the hopes and prayers of liberty loving people everywhere march with you". *The landings were yet another success. On August 7th, he set up his mobile headquarters at Maisons, then on August 9th at Jullouville. After the liberation of Paris, he led the battle of the Ardennes, the German campaign and the freeing of the camps. He then entered political life and became Republican President of the United States from 1952 to 1960. He was made docteur honoris causa of the University of Caen on November 13th 1948, the day the first stone was laid.*

Eisenhower roundabout at Bayeux.

and the first sub-prefect, Raymond Triboulet. Thus the chief of Free France affirmed his intention to assemble a French government and to thwart American aims to install their own administration: *"I want to make it clear immediately that every place abandoned by the Germans comes under the authority of my government"*. On the square dedicated to the chief of Free France there is a column with this inscription: *"On this spot on XIV June MCMXLIV / To the inhabitants of Bayeux / Joyful in their deliverance / Charles de Gaulle / Liberator of the Motherland / addressed his first words / on the soil of liberated France"*. This column recalls the intense joy of the inhabitants of Bayeux to be liberated.

Two years later, General de Gaulle returned to Bayeux and gave his famous

Poster about the arrival of de Gaulle in 1946.

De Gaulle in the main street of Bayeux.

speech in which he laid out the foundations of the Constitution of the Vth Republic. In June 1946, he declared: *"In our glorious but mutilated Normandy, Bayeux and its surroundings were witnesses to one the greatest clashes of history".* These days there is a memorial museum dedicated to General de Gaulle. It recounts the visits of the General to Bayeux through documents, photos, and film and sound tracks.

The biggest British cemetery in Normandy is to be found at Bayeux with 4,648 graves. On the other side of the Boulevard a monumental portico has been built, with the names of 1,807 missing soldiers.

The Memorial Museum of the Battle of Normandy stands at the official limit of the British and American sectors. This museum presents the Battle of Normandy chronologically and by theme. It traces precisely the whole human and military story with many documents, a hundred figures and several tons of equipment and material.

On the evening of D-Day, the soldiers of the Northumbrian attained their objective, to occupy the shore between Corseulles and Arromanches and reached the outskirts of Bayeux which was liberated the following day. At Creully they linked up with the Canadian soldiers who had landed on Juno Beach, but had to wait before they could join up

Portico of the British cemetery in Bayeux.

with the American soldiers in difficulty on Omaha Beach. While they were waiting for the artificial port of Arromanches to be built, the Allies held two small ports to receive supplies; Port-en-Bessin and Courseulles. On June 8th, the Americans and British linked up: thus two days after the landings, the Allies controlled about 38 miles of coast-line.

The Memorial Museum of the Battle of Normandy in Bayeux.

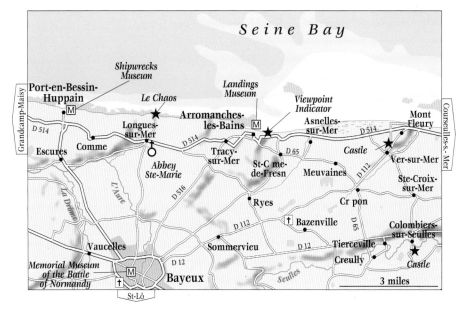

Omaha Beach

The first units of General Huebner, commander of the 1st infantry division nicknamed "the Big Red One" landed on the beaches leading to Sainte-Honorine-des-Pertes (Fox sector) up to the Percée point (Charlie sector). This division was made up of experienced soldiers who had fought in North Africa and Sicily. The sector was also that of the 29th infantry division, special engineers brigades and ranger battalions. Omar Bradley, commander of the 1st American army, supervised the landings from the cruiser *Augusta*. The mission of the American soldiers was to take up positions on 6,500 yards of beaches defined at each extremity by 100 ft high cliffs and to establish

themselves inland along a line Isigny-Trévières-Vaucelles, following the RN 13 road. The beaches of Colleville-sur-Mer, Saint-Laurent-sur-Mer and Vierville-sur-Mer were the only ones suitable for a disembarkment, as the Germans knew well, and consequently were well defended with small fortifications containing anti-tank weapons, 75 and 88 mm cannons and machine guns placed behind a variety of obstacles, land mines and barbed wire networks. They were dominated by chalk cliffs and valleys. On June 6th, the sea was particularly rough, which made it difficult for the landing craft and for launching the amphibious tanks.

Omaha Beach today.

Left page:
The 29th infantry division at Colleville-sur-Mer, June 6th 1944.

Landing operation, June 6th 1944, Omaha Beach. Drawing by Manuel Bromberg, an American artist in charge of illustrating the theatre of operations.

Arrival of the landing craft, June 6th 1944.

At 4.30 a.m., 180 barges (Landing Craft Infantry) were released at about five miles from the shore, but high seas sank several of them. The first ten ships sank but most of the soldiers were saved. As for their comrades, soaked, frozen and ill, they had to wait two hours longer before landing. While 29 Sherman DD (Duplex Drive nicknamed Donald Duck) amphibious tanks sank, the American troops tried to land under a deluge of German fire, caught under cross-fire from machine guns and mortars. They had to cross about 600 yards of beach to find shelter under the sea wall. As soon as the soldiers set foot on the beach, they came under heavy fire. The GI's fell, company after company. The war journal of the 116th regiment records: *"The enemy had awaited this moment. At the same time all our craft came under crossfire from its automatic weapons. Those men who instinctively jumped into*

Omaha landings,
June 6th 1944.

the water to avoid the fire drowned immediately. There was total disorder... However, several managed to stay at their stations. Many were wounded and drowned. Very few reached the shore". The German soldiers waited patiently in 85 little blockhouses which the GIs called pillboxes. The American general staff was unaware that the 352nd German infantry division, comprising elements from the eastern front, had chosen this sector for its manoeuvres, which doubled the German offensive. One hour after setting foot on the beach, the situation seemed alarming. The American soldiers could not advance. A report from the 5th army corps recorded a catastrophe at 7.30 a.m.: "Our assault units are collapsing under our eyes. We have very heavy losses. Enemy fire prevents us from taking the shore".

Dead and wounded on the beach. Drawing by Manuel Bromberg.

Bedford village in Virginia lost 23 men on June 6th, whereas it had only 3,000 inhabitants! Among them were the Hoback brothers, one killed and the other missing. Bedford is now twinned with Omaha Beach and plans to build a memorial.

Omaha Beach, a long beach of brown sand and pebbles bordered by a bank where yellow grasses grow became *Bloody Omaha* in only a few hours. At 9 a.m. the situation seemed so critical that General Omar Bradley considered abandoning the landing operations. Colonel George A. Taylor, commanding the 16th infantry regiment, noted: "*There are two sorts of men left on the beach! The dead and those about to die! Let's get out of here, fast*". Then Omar Bradley ordered the fleet to bombard the German defences again. This vital decision enabled the soldiers to finally move forward, especially since the Germans were beginning to run out of ammunition. The sappers were particularly courageous and managed to clear a large part of the beach. After several hours of fighting, they managed to establish a fragile bridgehead about a mile deep but at the price of 3,000 killed and just as many wounded or disappeared in the waves.

Opposite:
Omaha, June 6th 1944.

General Omar Bradley (1893-1981)

Second-in-command to Eisenhower in North Africa in 1943 and greatly respected by his soldiers, he commanded the 11th army corps in Tunisia and Sicily, and then the 1st army during the landings. He was a good tactician, and organised Operation Cobra. On August 1st, he was promoted to head the 12th American armies group in Germany. He was later named Chief of Staff of the United States armies. He retired in 1953. He published his Memoirs, "A soldier's story", in 1952.

Sainte-Honorine-des-Pertes

This commune, situated at the eastern end of Omaha, was subject to a reconnaissance raid during the night of September 12th to 13th 1942 within the framework of Operation Aquatint, but the twelve agents from the Secret Operation Executive making up the commando were killed. Despite the difficulties of the Omaha landings, the commune was liberated on June 7th. At the beginning of July, its little port was one of the destinations of PLUTO in order to provide fuel for the American armies. This pipeline, called "Minor system", linked up with that from Port-en-Bessin and was connected to Saint-Lô through the "Major system" coming from the port of Cherbourg.

Monument for the 1st ID at Colleville-sur-Mer.

Colleville-sur-Mer

This small town was severely shelled until it was liberated on June 7th at about 10 a.m. after house-to-house fighting. The 1st and 29th infantry divisions took a foothold there at the

Monumental statue, American cemetery at Colleville-sur-Mer.

price of thousands of dead, wounded or missing on the beach defended by the "Plus-kat" fortifications. A monument dedicated to the 5th engineers brigade has been erected on the remains of a blockhouse. Above this there is an obelisk monument in honour of the 1st American infantry division.

These days, the tranquillity of the beach, owned by the Coast Conservatory, is in stark contrast to the horrors of D-Day.

But this commune and that of Saint-Laurent-sur-Mer became world known because of the American cemetery built by *the American battle monuments commission*. It was inaugurated in 1956 by the President of the Republic, René Coty, and General Marshall; the site covers 175 acres and has been given to the American government for perpetuity on the cliff overlooking Omaha Beach. This was the battleground of the right wing of the 1st infantry division. There were 9,386 American soldiers killed in Normandy and buried there; among them 307 unknown soldiers. The thousands of graves in white Carrare marble aligned perfectly on a trimmed lawn give the impression of greatness and beauty. The remembrance stones

are in the shape of a Latin cross or the star of David. A father and son lie together and there are thirty-three cases of brothers buried together.

A circular chapel has been built out of Vaurion (Côte-d'Or) stone with steps in Ploumanac'h granite (Côtes-d'Armor). The frieze is decorated with a replica of the Congress medal and the altar is in Pyrenean marble. Above the altar, the grateful French have placed a crown of laurels for the soldiers who died for the Freedom of Europe. The roof mosaic, made by Léon Kroll from New York, symbolises America blessing its sons, going to war. A time capsule containing newspaper articles from June 6th 1944 is enclosed there and will only be opened on June 6th 2044.

The memorial represents a semi-circular series of columns in Vaurion stone; in the centre there is a monumental bronze statue 23 feet high created by Donald de Lue. It symbolises the spirit of American youth emerging from the waves and carries the inscription: "My eyes have seen the glory of the coming of the Lord". To the left of this monument is a belvedere overlooking the beach: a panoramic table shows the general map of the landings and explains the fighting for Omaha Beach.

There is a wall dedicated to the Missing in the garden in the form of an arc of a circle with 1,557

Colleville-sur-Mer beach.

The American cemetery.

names. Not far away there is a pool with two flagpoles. A granite staircase gives a view of the cliffs, Omaha Beach and the Pointe du Hoc.

Homage to the German soldiers of the 716th infantry division killed in Omaha is marked by a cross at point WN 62.

Remnants on the cliff overlooking Omaha Beach.

January 17th to 18th 1942. Paradoxically, this beach was called Easy Beach for landing operations while in fact it was a very difficult spot to win. A lieutenant shouted to his men: "*Are you going to stay there to be killed or are you going to get up and try not to be killed?*"

The village was liberated at 1 p.m. on June 6th. Not far from the "Les Moulins" hamlet, where there is a commemorative stone, there still remains a blockhouse which served as the first headquarters in charge of organising the first exchanges between the beach and inland. In front, there is a monument commemorating the landing of the 2nd "Indian Head" infantry division on June 7th. A memorial dedicated to the same division has been built on the Ruquet site. The first American airstrip was built near Saint-Laurent in order to evacuate the wounded.

On the sea-front, just like on most of the landing beaches, there is a memorial monument dedicated to this event and built by the Landings Committee.

The June 6th 1944 Omaha museum shows a collection of uniforms, vehicles, weapons and emblems. One can see a 155 mm cannon given by the United States Defence Ministry.

The Dog Red and Dog White sectors were established between Saint-Laurent-sur-Mer and Vierville-sur-Mer: it was here that General Norman Cota managed to link up men from different companies scattered by the tough fighting and to launch another assault on the German defences.

Saint-Laurent-sur-Mer

Just like the other beaches of Calvados, that of Saint-Laurent-sur-Mer was subject to a reconnaissance raid by fifteen men during the night of

Omaha Museum.

*Signal-memorial
at Saint-Laurent-sur-Mer.*

Vierville-sur-Mer

This sector of Omaha, called Dog Green, was the most deadly and the most confused. Not only did the landing craft sink with all their men aboard, but the tanks were hit by fire from the cannons from Percée Point. Only a third of the 180 soldiers of the A company were able to continue while all their officers had been killed. The village was liberated at 11 a.m. on June 6th. At the far end of the road along the beach there remains a German pillbox, one of the defensive points which pre-vented the American soldiers from leaving the beach. These days the blockhouse has a monument on top dedicated to the American National Guard in memory of its participation in two World Wars.

Elements of the jetty of the Mulberry A artificial port are still visible at low tide. This port, built on June 8th, was destroyed during the storm which hit the coasts between June 19th and 22nd. Eight hundred ships ran aground on the beaches. The sea's caprices delayed all the disembarkment operations; Bradley's troops were running

National Guard at Vierville-sur-Mer.

Storm over the Mulberries.

out of ammunition and the offensive planned for the 22nd on the Odon had to be postponed. Despite the damage, what remained of the artificial port made it possible to land 600,000 men and 104,000 vehicles before February 28th 1945. Some of the debris was used to repair the Arromanches artificial port.

A small monument below the road recalls that Vierville-sur-Mer was the site of the first American cemetery. It carries this inscription: "This marks the site of the first American cemetery in France of World War II, since moved to American cemetery No. 1". The many dead on Omaha Beach were first of all buried in the sand and then, from June 19th, transferred to the Colleville-sur-Mer cemetery.

The village was taken on June 6th and the castle served as headquarters for the American army from June 8th to July 21st.

Englesqueville-la-Percée

The coast road leads the visitor to this village which had a big radar station named Igel in charge of watching the seas. The station was built on Percée Point, a rocky spur similar to the Pointe du Hoc. It comprised a Freya-type radar specialised in marine surveillance plus two enormous Würzburg-type radars.

After May 1944, these radars were silenced by the bombardments. The whole ensemble was captured by the 2nd rangers battalion on June 7th. Taking the fortified stronghold defended by two 77 mm cannons was especially difficult; only 29 of the 70 rangers managed to reach the top of the cliff. They needed support from naval artillery to silence the cannons at about 1.00 p.m. on June 6th. When the rangers reached the fortifications in the evening, they found the bodies of 69 German soldiers.

Pointe du Hoc

After passing Saint-Pierre-du-Mont where the German battery was bombarded in the afternoon of June 5th and neutralised on the 7th, the visitor reaches this splendid site of about 30 acres with its rocky prow pointing out to sea. The cliff, 100 feet high, had been thoroughly fortified by the Germans who had installed a battery there equipped with six French-origin 155 mm cannons on huge circular platforms open to the sky. This arrangement meant that the cannons could fire in any direction. Their fire, directed by an observation post at the edge of the cliff, had a range of 12 miles and could reach the east coast of the Cotentin peninsula. The German garrison was guarded by 125 infantry and

Pointe du Hoc, view of the cliff.

80 gunners protected by machine guns and well shielded in bunkers linked up by communication passages behind the barbed wire and the mines. The Todt organisation had begun building concrete pillboxes to house the cannons but the work was not finished in June 1944.

Aerial view of the Pointe du Hoc.

Rangers climbing the Pointe du Hoc.

bombing during the night of June 5th to 6th: 700 tons of bombs were dropped by 124 planes in only a few minutes, while from the sea came a deluge of bombs and shells. The battleship *Texas*, in particular, fired over 600 salvoes of 356! The rangers had been specially trained for assault on the cliffs of the Isle of Wight, using grappling irons, ropes, extensible rope ladders and even telescopic ladders lent by London's firemen. On June 6th at 7.10 a.m. 225 rangers in three separate companies, landed at the bottom of the cliff of the Pointe du Hoc which the Allies called "Ho Point" on their maps. But the rangers had their ropes cut by the German defenders and came under machine-gun fire and hand grenades; 135 of the 225 were put out of action during the attack. The situation remained uncertain for 48 hours and it was only on June 8th at about midday that the battery was taken by the rangers.

The rangers had studied the site on aerial photos, but when they arrived they could not recognise anything since the terrain had been changed so much by the shelling and piles of concrete rubble.

The final victory came with the support of the 116th infantry regiment to which the ranger battalion belonged, backed up by tanks. The site, which has been kept in the state it was, remains marked by the ferocity of the fighting, but this victory was

This stronghold was taken by storm by the 2nd battalion of rangers commanded by Colonel James Rudder. The attack had been prepared by

The shambles of the zone.

Remains of a pillbox.

James Rudder

James Rudder, nicknamed "Big Jim", was a farmer, played American football and then became a trainer in Texas. From June 1943 he commanded the 2nd rangers battalion. He won glory at the Pointe du Hoc and the DSC medal for his courage. He was later promoted Brigadier General and received the Légion d'Honneur. After the war he was elected President of the University of Texas.

useless since the cannons had been dismantled several days before and replaced by big timber beams! The six cannons were hidden several miles away in an orchard behind apple trees.

Today this is a 60 acre site protected by the Coastline Conservation Trust, and the gaping funnel-shaped holes and destroyed blockhouses are still to be seen.

The path leading to the edge of the cliff is now called "Colonel Rudder Alley". German and American bodies still lie under the rubble.

The land has been conceded to the American government and has become a military sanctuary. At the very tip of the Point a monument has been built in the shape of a simple granite needle on the very site of the former firing direction post. On a cross planted in the earth one reads the following inscription: "Here the combatants remain. In its chaos, the battle united them for eternity".

TO THE HEROIC RANGER COMMANDOES
D 2 RN E 2 RN F 2 RN
OF THE 116TH INF
WHO UNDER THE COMMAND OF
COLONEL JAMES E. RUDDER
OF THE FIRST AMERICAN DIVISION
ATTACKED AND TOOK POSSESSION OF
THE POINTE DU HOC

Monuments on the Pointe du Hoc.

View of the Cotentin peninsula.

*Monument to the American
National Guard
at Grandcamp-Maisy.*

Grandcamp-Maisy

At very low tide the sea uncovers a vast plateau of chalk rocks called the Roches de Grandcamp, extending for 5 miles from the Pointe du Hoc to the beginning of Veys Bay. The village of Grandcamp-les-Bains, turned into a defensive stronghold by the Germans, was liberated on June 9th. General Bradley set up the headquarters of the 1st American army there and General Eisenhower stayed there from July 1st to 5th.

The village of Maisy, located further away from the coast, was defended by the batteries of La Martinière and La Perruque. These two batteries controlled the estuary of the river Vire, one with three 100 mm cannons and the other with six 155 mm cannons with a range of 12 miles. They were a direct threat to the sector of Utah on the east coast of the Cotentin peninsula, and were put out of action

in the afternoon of June 6th by the cruiser *Hawkins* and were occupied on June 9th.

There is a rangers museum paying homage to their action. Just on entering the commune one finds a monument dedicated to the National Guard.

La Cambe

First of all, this village was the site of an American cemetery with 4,534 graves which later were transferred to the United States or to the Colleville-sur-Mer cemetery. These days, extending over 5 acres, there is a German cemetery with 21,202 graves. One enters through a porch which also acts as a chapel. Each soldier's name is inscribed on a small stone set in the closely-mowed lawn. The stone crosses are in groups of five on the grass. In the middle of the cemetery there is a tumulus 20 feet high topped by a granite cross with two statues at its sides: it contains the bodies of 296 non-identified German soldiers.

Isigny-sur-Mer

This town was supposed to be taken on June 6th, but the German defenders resisted along the RN 13 road. On June 9th the taking of this important milk industry centre at the back of Veys Bay by the 29th American infantry division, allowed the Omaha and Utah sectors to be linked up. But this only happened at the price of heavy bombing and great destruction, the town being 60% destroyed. Omar Bradley declared: "*The people of Isigny had waited for more than four years to be liberated. And now, seeing the ruins of their country, they consider us as responsible*". On General-de-Gaulle Square, in the middle of the town, a monument set up by the Landings Committee recalls the speech the head of Free France pronounced to the population on June 14th.

By the evening of June 6th, the Americans had lost over 3,000 soldiers, but 30,000 were established in a narrow bridgehead 1 1/4 miles inland whereas 6 1/4 had been planned! The

powerful and efficient Naval artillery out at sea moved in to 800 yards from the shore and managed to unblock a situation which Bradley had thought compromised at one time. The site of Omaha Beach will always remain the most tragic, as shown by the American cemetery of Colleville/Saint-Laurent. Omar Bradley holds up his soldiers as an example: *"Each man who set foot on Omaha Beach that day was a hero"*. Luckily, the following days saw an improvement: on June 8th the American soldiers linked up with their British colleagues who had landed at Gold Beach.

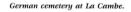

German cemetery at La Cambe.

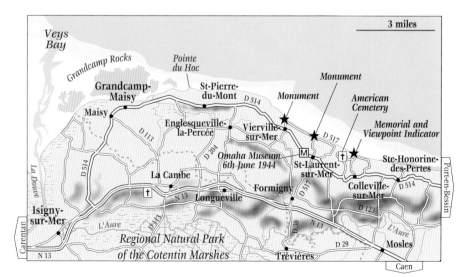

U t a h   B e a c h

This was the fifth and final landing sector of D-Day, and the second American sector, but the only one situated in the département of Manche. The mission of the 7th army corps, commanded by General J. L. Collins, was to take the coastal positions and establish a solid bridgehead. That of the 4th infantry division of General R. O. Barton, whose second-in-command was General Teddy Roosevelt, was to establish themselves on the roads on the embankments above the flooded land and to link up with the 82nd and the 101st airborne divisions parachuted after midnight over Sainte-Mère-Eglise. The 101st had the task of clearing the terrain between the sea and Sainte-Mère-Eglise whilst the 82nd was to take this town and the bridges over the Merderet and the Douve rivers. In order to protect Utah Beach, the American paratroopers quickly took the Varreville dunes. Once these positions had been established, the American troops which had landed in the Utah and Omaha sectors linked up and in ten days advanced towards Cherbourg, about 30 miles away.

The Utah sector had a special role to play in Operation Overlord. If the landing operations failed on one of these beaches or even on all, the general staff had planned to send everyone to this sector. The mission was to cut the Cotentin peninsula in two.

Therefore the Utah landing had to succeed. The landing took place at 6.30 a.m. but 1 1/4 miles further south than intended. It was the least bloody of all the five sectors, with only 200 dead, since the attack had been well prepared by aerial bombing followed by fire from the warships. The ensemble of the sector was defended by five batteries, one of them very powerful, at Saint-Marcouf, and by a certain number of small fortifications at Saint-Martin-de-Varreville, Audouville-la-Hubert, La Madeleine, Beau Guillot and Le Grand Vey. At about 2 a.m. a thousand ships carrying 30,000 men and 3,500 vehicles approached the beaches of the eastern coast of Cotentin.

Left page:
Landing at Utah, June 6th 1944.

The peaceful beach today.

The church of Sainte-Mère-Eglise.

Sainte-Mère-Eglise

The bell-tower with its dummy figure.

The "Screaming Eagles" airborne emblem.

On June 6th, at about 1 a.m., 15,000 paratroopers from the 82nd and 101st airborne divisions, commanded respectively by Generals Matthew B. Ridgeway and Maxwell D. Taylor, were dropped above and around this town. The former had had experience of Sicily and Salerno, while the latter were inexperienced.

But the parachute drop was not precise enough, so much so that only 6,000 soldiers were in a position to fight. Many were scattered, for example General Maxwell Taylor. The furthest away landed near Barfleur, but others were drowned, tangled in their parachutes or sinking under the weight of the heavy equipment they were carrying. The survivors found each other using a little metallic toy imitating the song of the grasshopper. Unfortunately for some soldiers, the sound was similar to that of the German Mauser rifle!

By sending its reserves to look for the scattered paratroopers, the German general staff made the landing on the beach easier. The paratroopers of the 82nd airborne were more precise than their comrades of the 101st; three quarters of them landed within a square of 3 miles. They managed to take Sainte-Mère-Eglise, defended by the 91st division of the Luftwaffe at 4.30 a.m., that is two hours before the landing. This conquest made it pos-

sible to cut the RN 13 road between
Carentan and Cherbourg. The American flag which floated that night at
Sainte-Mère-Eglise was the same
which had earlier floated over
Naples. The paratroopers then
unhooked their comrade John Steele
who was still caught by his parachute
on the steeple of the church and who
was wounded by German fire. These
days there is a dummy figure attached to the church to recall this
event.

Inside the church there are stained glass windows showing the arrival of the paratroops at Sainte-
Mère-Eglise. The window above
the portal representing the paratroopers around the Virgin Mary is
the work of master glass-maker
Loire based on drawings by Paul
Renaud.

This town sheltered the first American cemeteries: cemetery No. 1 with
2,195 graves and cemetery No. 2 with
4,811 graves. In the latter, Brigadier
General Roosevelt was buried on July
14th. Later, these dead were transferred to Colleville-sur-Mer or repatria-
ted to the United States.

In memory of the actions of the
American 82nd and 101st airborne
divisions, a paratrooper museum has
been built near the church. Among
other equipment, one can see a Waco-
type glider there. The first stone of
the building, whose roof is in the
shape of a parachute, was laid by
General Gavin in 1962. A neighbouring dome-shaped building contains a
Dakota C 47.

Stained glass window in the church.

Museum of Airborne Troops.

73

Milestone 00 at La Madeleine.

Milestone 0 leads from the town hall of Saint-Mère-Eglise to the "Liberty Highway", inaugurated on September 16th 1947. Milestone 00 is on Utah Beach and leads to La Madeleine to link up with Bastogne, 715 miles away.

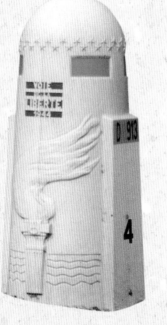

Vierville milestone.

These milestones symbolically mark the itinerary of the American army as it advanced towards the liberation of Europe and led to Bastogne in Belgium. These milestones can be divided between four sectors:

— sector 1 from Sainte-Mère-Eglise to Cherbourg (milestone 58). The Cherbourg stone is set at the junction of the France and Normandy quays;

— sector 2 from Sainte-Mère-Eglise to Avranches via Carentan, Saint-Lô and Villedieu-les-Poêles;

— sector 3 from Avranches to Metz:

— sector 4 from Metz to Bastogne.

Not far from Sainte-Mère-Eglise, the commune of Vierville was also liberated on June 6th.

Remnants on the beach.

Sainte-Marie-du-Mont

This old town, dominated by its Norman church, was occupied very early on by the paratroopers of the 101st Airborne led by General Maxwell Taylor. The Madeleine beach has become famous under the name of Utah Beach. A stained glass window in the church recalls the episodes liberating the village on June 6th.

On June 6th at 6.30 a.m. the 4th American infantry division landed by error on the "Grande Dune" hamlet, whereas the landing was planned for more than a mile to the north, facing the Varreville sand-dunes. General Theodore Roosevelt then aged 57 years and cousin of the President of the United States, walking with a stick, landed with the first wave and decided to continue operations. He justified his presence by telling General Barton: *"It will reassure the boys to know that I am with them"*. The La Madeleine sector was one of the least defended, which not only made the landings easy for the men but also for the equipment. Therefore, the 33 ton Sherman DD tanks could go into action quickly while the engineers' bulldozers cleaned the beach. The Germans were severely hit by preventive bombardments: they tried to send Goliath miniature tanks filled with explosives, but only one exploded. A huge obelisk, erected thanks to the sub-

1st special engineers brigade monument.

scription of veterans of the American 4th infantry division, commemorates the action of these soldiers near the remnants of the German pillboxes. Close by, a column in pink granite, 30 feet high, was erected by

the *"United States of America in honour of its profound gratitude to its sons who gave their lives for the liberation of these beaches on June 6th 1944"*. This column was inaugurated on June 5th 1984 by General J. L. Collins. There is also a third monument dedicated to the soldiers of the 1st special engineers brigade.

Following a suggestion of General Gaffey, 59 panels remembering the dead of this engineers brigade have been placed where they were killed.

Finally, a memorial stone recalls the landing of the 90th infantry division.

90th infantry division monument.

Monument to the American 1st special engineers brigade.

Beau Guillot pillbox.

Landings museum,
Sainte-Marie-du-Mont.

There is a Landings museum in a blockhouse of the Atlantic Wall.

Each of the streets of this hamlet is named after soldiers or officers killed on June 6th; there is a stained glass window in the chapel made by the stained-glass artist Pierre Marie dedicated to Sainte Madeleine, which evokes the French forces inland: *"In the year 1944, the Free French forces took part in the landings with the Allied troops".*

On the road from La Madeleine to Sainte-Marie-du-Mont one can see a monument, the work of the Danish sculptor Svend Lindhart, dedicated to the 800 Danish sailors who took part in the landings. The fortifications of Beau Guillot remain at about 1/2 mile from La Madeleine.

Poupeville

This tiny hamlet, neighbouring Sainte-Marie-du-Mont, sheltered a German command post which supplied the strongholds of the sector.

Gliders crashed at Hiesville.

Pillbox at Beau Guillot.

Therefore, it was vital to take it, as Gilles Perrault emphasises. The capture was relatively late because the paratroopers in charge had been scattered. Local resistance had prepared for their assault by cutting the telephone cables. The men of the 101st left Hiesville at 6 a.m. and controlled the hamlet by midday. The Poupeville bridge was the point where the airborne troops and those who had landed on La Madeleine beach that morning linked up.

Hiesville

This village, about 4 miles from Sainte-Mère-Eglise, was liberated on June 6th by the paratroopers of the 101st, backed up by 32 Waco gliders. The latter brought in the reinforcements and equipment needed to consolidate their positions. Some gliders crashed on Rommel's stakes. A hospital was set up in the Colom-bières manor. A temporary cemetery was built there before being transferred to the neighbouring commune of Blosville.

Blosville

This village, liberated on June 7th, sheltered a temporary cemetery of 5,622 graves of American soldiers, victims of the terrible and deadly war of the hedges. These bodies were later transferred to the Colleville-sur-Mer cemetery.

Picauville-Chef-du-Pont

Chef-du-Pont was one of the priorities of the 82nd airborne with the taking of the Merderet bridge and was conquered after three days of fighting, on June 9th. The Luftwaffe 91st division had installed its tactical command post in Picauville castle. But its commander, General Falley, who had left for Rennes but

*The Americans
entering Carentan.*

*Ruins of pillboxes
on Varreville beach.*

the strong currents due to the bad weather, and arrived on the La Madeleine beach. Near this offshore bar, the villagers of Saint-Martin-de-Varreville saw the landing of General Leclerc and his 2nd armoured division of 15,000 men and 4,000 vehicles. A monument in pink granite in the shape of a ship's prow with the emblem of the Cross of Lorraine recalls this landing. Near the monument there are two vehicles carrying the emblem of the 2nd DB.

The coastal road called the Allies Road passes the Utah Beach sector. The dunes were defended by several batteries. That of Saint-Martin-de-

returned, was killed in his car on June 6th by three American paratroopers.

Amfréville

The 82nd Airborne chose the zone surrounding this village for their landing, but the flooding of the marshes made it difficult. The paratroopers were scattered and had enormous difficulty in meeting each other with their "grasshoppers". The village was only liberated on June 12th after fierce fighting.

Carentan

This town is the only point in the Manche département where it was possible to cross the marshes towards Bessin, by the Grand Vey ford. It was only liberated by the 101st Airborne on June 12th. The town was bombarded in the morning of June 6th and again in the afternoon. On June 10th the American soldiers tried in vain to cross the four bridges. The taking of the town was marked by terrible fighting on the Carentan highway and the square of Choux when the 502nd airborne division advanced along the old RN 13 road.

The Vareville dunes

This site should have been that of Utah Beach, but the landing craft were 1 1/4 miles away because of

Varreville, comprising four 105 mm cannons, was bombarded in the night of June 5th to 6th, but the guns had been dismantled. The battery was quickly taken by American soldiers.

The naval battery of Crisbecq (named after the hamlet) at Saint-Marcouf, the biggest in the Seine bay after that of Le Havre, comprised four 210 mm cannons with a range of 17 miles, but only three were in working order. Their fire-power was able to sink an American destroyer on June 7th. The battery covered a sector from Veys Bay to Saint-Vaast-la-Hougue. The ensemble as a whole was defended by a garrison of

400 men equipped with cannons and machine guns. All around there were anti-tank obstacles, mines and barbed wire. As Rémy Desquesnes noted, Crisbecq was the centre of gravity of German defences on the Cotentin eastern coast but, as a result, was bombed the most. This battery, overlooking the beaches of Ravenoville and Saint-Germain-de-Varreville, resisted all the bombing and different assaults of the American paratroops and the American 4th division until June 12th when the Germans decided to withdraw. One can still see there a huge shelter for a 210 mm cannon. However, most of the pillboxes were destroyed by specialists from the engineers: they exploded them to test possible weaknesses of these constructions.

At "Les Campagnettes" hamlet, 2 1/2 miles from the sea, was the Azeville battery, comprising four 105 mm cannons with a range of 6 miles. It acted as back-up for the Crisbecq battery. It was taken by flame-throwers on June 9th by soldiers of the 22nd infantry regiment. These days one can see two cells with a cistern on top to shelter a cannon.

Ravenoville pillbox.

Quinéville

This town marked the northern limit of the Utah sector, but also the extreme point of the American Cotentin advance by the evening of June 15th. The King of England James II left from here to take part in the battle of the Hougue in 1692. During the night of December 25th to 26th 1943, this beach of fine sand had been visited by a British reconnaissance commando. It was defended by the Morsalines battery

Ruins of pillboxes at Crisbecq.

equipped with six 155 mm cannons. Bombed by Allied planes, it was evacuated by the Germans and its guns moved 1 1/4 miles away. This new position meant that the cannons could not reach the La Madeleine beach which was now too far away. The beach was cleared on June 15th after taking the Saint-Marcouf fort.

The Freedom Museum recreates the atmosphere of life under the Occupation through models, photos of the time and daily objects.

Remains of pillboxes at Azeville.

By the evening of June 6th, the Americans had landed 23,500 men, 1,700 vehicles and 1,800 tons of supplies. Despite several centres of resistance such as Quinéville or the Saint-Marcouf and Azeville positions, a solid bridgehead had been established and the link-up with the 82nd and 101st airborne divisions had been made. The German defences in the Utah sector put up little resistance, so that about midday on June 6th General Bradley received a reassuring message: *"Beaches cleaned, routes under construction, little opposition"*. It remained for all these American armies to start advancing towards the north of the département with the aim of cutting off the Cotentin peninsula and above all to take Cherbourg. The

beaches of the Utah sector, sheltered from any German counter-attack, saw the landing of 836,000 men from forty divisions, 220,000 vehicles and 725,000 tons of supplies between the months of June and November 1944.

3 miles

Quinéville

D 25

D 42

D 421

Cherbourg

N 13

Montebourg

D 14

Crisbec

St-Marcouf

D 14

D 421

Azeville

Ravenoville

D 15

St-Germain-
de-Varreville

Les Dunes

D 14

St-Martin-
de-Varreville

N 13

Merderet

D 67

D 421

D 128

Amfreville

Airborne Troops
Museum

La Madeleine

D 15

M

D 15

D 115

D 913

Beau Guillot

M

Ste-Mère-Église

D 329

DC 47
Douglas Museum

D 14

D 15

Merderet

Pont-l'Abbé

D 70

D 70

Pouppeville

Picauville

Chef-du-Pont

M

D 115

Ste-Marie-
du-Mont

D 67

Hiesville

Blosville

N 13

Douve

Vierville

D 913

Canal from Carentan to the Sea

Regional Natural Park
of the Cotentin Marshes

St-Côme-
du-Mont

Douve

Brévands

Sèves

D 89

Bayeux

D 903

N 13

Carentan

N 174

D 903

D 223

D 971

N 13

St-Lô

Central and Southern Manche

Capturing Cherbourg was of very great importance because of the strategic and logistic interests of the port. Once this mission was accomplished, by General Lawton Collins, on June 26th 1944, the American troops disembarked all the equipment, material and supplies they needed to continue their operations. For his part, General Omar Bradley drew up Operation Cobra. The aim was to leave the marshlands and break through the German front in the direction of Avranches. The American divisions were held back by the war of the hedges from the end of June. They attacked in order to break through the German defences from July 25th, with heavy shelling which destroyed many towns and villages.

The war of the hedges

The bushy hedges, thick copses, small hunting grounds, banks, ditches and narrow paths which criss-crossed the wooded landscape of the centre and south of Manche, were completely new to the American troops, most of them young inexperienced recruits. On the other hand, the German soldiers knew these copses and pastures well since they had been there for four years. Each hedge, each copse, and each path represented a natural trap which made bloody guerrilla warfare possible. The German defences were organised into three lines: automatic weapons for the first, mortars for the second, and cannons for the third. Four American army corps were involved in this hedges hell: the 7th led by General Collins between Carentan and Périers, the 5th commanded by General Gerow to the east of Saint-Lô, the 8th of General Middleton between La Haye-du-Puits and Coutances and the 19th under General Corlett between the Vire and Taute rivers in the Saint-Lô direction. The modern weapons of the American soldiers were ineffective: the shells were not able to pierce these hedges made up of bushy trees and thick scrub. The tanks had great difficulty in moving and manoeuvring. Every time a tank tried to climb a bank it became an easy target for the enemy. Besides this, the continuing bad weather of summer 1944 turned the land into an impracticable quag-

Left page: **Saint-Lô in ruins. Painting by Pierre Campain, 1946.**

American soldiers in the hedges.

85

Convoy in the ruins of Saint-Lô.

*American soldiers
in the hedges.*

mire. In fact, only the infantrymen managed to advance in what became the hell of the hedges. But their progress was very slow and systematic, advancing field after field, orchard after orchard, hedge after hedge: the 8th army corps battled for twelve days and only moved 7 miles forward! The soldiers advanced without knowing where the enemy was, and exposed themselves to deadly enemy fire. Finally, the tanks were made more effective thanks to the idea of an American sergeant who fixed a sort of steel cutting plough to the front of the tank. This improvement turned the tank into a bulldozer, nicknamed "Rhinoceros", which could knock down the hedges and copses and flatten the banks. In mid-July, the four American armies stopped their slow progress, since it was costing too many lives: for a gain of 3 miles, the 8th army corps lost 5,000 men; as for the 19th army corps, for a

gain of 6 miles it lost 6,000 men. The only town which was taken was La-Haye-du-Puits after seven days of fierce fighting. This hell of the hedges lasted for more than four weeks until Operation Cobra, launched on July 25th, and its carpet bombing managed to free the bogged-down American armies and broke through the German front.

Marigny - La Chapelle-Enjuger

In the night of June 5th to 6th, in order to attract the attention of the Germans, the Royal Air Force parachuted dummies filled with sand over Rampan, Marigny and the Lessay heath. On June 13th, the commune of Marigny was bombed and destroyed. When Operation Cobra was launched on July 25th, it attacked the front line. Sixty thousand tons of fragmentation, napalm or phosphorus bombs were dropped by more than 1,600 flying for-

tresses and 1,500 fighter-bombers, flattening the villages of La Chapelle-Enjuger, Hébécrevon, Saint-Gilles and Mesnil-Eury over an area of only 4 square miles. The Panzer Lehr was crushed under the bombs, as its commander General Bayerlein stated: *My front line looked like a lunar landscape and at least 70% of my men were put out of action, dead, wounded or in a state of shock".* After being liberated on July 27th, a temporary American cemetery was built sheltering 3,024 graves until the Colleville-sur-Mer cemetery was created. Not far away, 4,000 German soldiers were buried in mass graves until the creation of a permanent cemetery in the communes of Marigny and La Chapelle-Enjuger: it contains 11,169 graves.

Périers - Coutances

Operation Cobra destroyed towns and villages in its wake: Périers was

80% destroyed and Coutances 65%. Coutances had already been flattened twice by bombing, on June 6th and June 12th. The town burned for several days. On July 26th, the road leading from Saint-Lô to Coutances was cut by the Americans at Saint-Gilles. Périers and Lessay were liberated on July 27th and Coutances the following day.

Saint-Lô

On June 6th the town was bombed. It came under 5,000 tons of bombs and was 90% destroyed: it became the "capital of ruins". In fact, Saint-Lô was a vital communications centre and the command post of the 84th German army Korps. During the bombardment of the 6th, the prison was destroyed, causing the death of 42 resistants including the sub-prefect of Cherbourg, Lionel Audigier.

In the morning of June 7th, Saint-Lô was in ruins, but still controlled by the Germans, who turned it into a resistance outpost to counter the American advance. On July 12th the American soldiers were halted on the heights surrounding the town and on the road linking Saint-Lô to Lessay. On July 17th the Americans captured Pont-Hébert and occupied the hills overlooking Saint-Lô. On July 18th, the 115th American regiment entered the town despite heavy losses. The fighting continued among the ruins for a whole week. On July 25th, General Bradley launched Operation Cobra: the Panzer Lehr front

American soldiers entering Saint-Lô.

87

Major Howie Square in Saint-Lô.

Major Thomas D. Howie, born in Virginia in 1908

As Operations Officer of the 29th American infantry division, he landed at Omaha. He took part in the battle of Saint-Lô and was killed in the evening of July 18th by a shell exploding. He was wrapped in the American flag and carried to the ruins of the Sainte-Croix church by his men. He became the symbol of the American victims and their sacrifices during the terrible battle for the liberation of Saint-Lô. The American poet Joseph Auslander dedicated a poem to him 'Incident at St-Lô': "They carried him, upright, proud and grave, through the gates of St-Lô".

Beaucoudray monument.

to the south of the Périers - Saint-Lô road was wiped out under carpet bombing.

Although they had intended to capture the town a week after landing, the Americans did not enter it until forty-three days later. But this hard-won victory allowed General Patton to launch the attack on Avranches on the 26th of July.

When the visitor arrives from Bayeux, he comes to a roundabout dedicated to Major Howie. His bronze bust symbolises the sacrifices of these thousands of GIs who fought to liberate the town.

Beaucoudray

Between Villebaudon and Beaucoudray, at the "Ferme du Bois", the

Post Office resistance unit of Saint-Lô took refuge. Carelessness meant that they were detected by a group of SS soldiers stationed nearby. After a short period of fighting, 11 resistants were captured on June 14th and shot the next day in a field where a monument has been erected.

Avranches

Avranches, famous for its library and its rich collection of manuscripts from the abbey of Mont-Saint-Michel, was bombarded for three days, on June 7th, 8th and 10th. On July 30th, a hundred German vehicles trying to counter-attack were destroyed by Allied bombing. The same day, Bréhal, Gavray, La Haye-Pesnel and Sartilly were liberated. General Patton's 3rd army took the Germans from behind and liberated Avranches on July 30th and 31st after a quick breakthrough. Even though he only held a single bridge, Patton managed to pass seven divisions in three days. He could therefore enter Brittany and reached Rennes on August 4th.

American tanks entering Avranches on July 31st 1944.

89

George Patton (1885-1945)

George Patton was nicknamed "Blood and guts" by his soldiers, both because of his courage and his brutality.
He was trained at the armoured cavalry school of West Point, and fought Pancho Villa in 1916. He was appointed aide-de-camp to General Pershing during the First World War. Insisting on fighting with tanks, he showed great audacity during the landing in Northern Africa in 1942 and commanded the 7th division in Sicily.
But, after slapping a soldier, he fell into disgrace and colleague Bradley was chosen to lead the fighting in Normandy. He was given the command of the phantom army during Operation Fortitude before being called to Normandy in July 1944. On August 1st, his 3rd army entered into the battle with the breakthrough to Avranches and then advanced on Paris and the Ardennes.
In March 1945, he was at Trèves and then entered Austria and Czechoslovakia: he burst into tears when he discovered the concentration camps.
He was appointed governor of Bavaria and then relieved of his post because of his anti-Soviet attitude. He published his Memoirs "War as I knew it", and died in a car accident on December 21st 1945.

A monument dedicated to General Patton has been built on the very spot where he stayed. This park is American territory: the soil and the trees were brought from America.

A Second World War museum, at Val-Saint-Père, recounts the breakthrough into Avranches. The ground floor shows the German side whilst the first floor is devoted to the Allied side. This museum holds the bell which sounded the alarm on June 6th on the Pointe du Hoc.

Saint-James

This village, liberated on the same day as Pontorson and Tessy-sur-Vire, shelters one of the two American cemeteries in Lower Normandy. In a setting of greenery stretching over 30 acres, 1 1/4 miles to the south-east, lie 4,410 soldiers from the 3rd American army. The little marble crosses are dominated by a chapel with a steeple on top. In this memorial chapel one finds a collection of flags, stained glass windows, emblems and maps representing the events of 1944.

Huisnes-sur-Mer

Overlooking the bay a few miles from the abbey of Mont-Saint-Michel, which was miraculously preserved from the destruction of the war, is a German ossuary. There are 68 cavities which have contained the remains of 11,956 soldiers since 1963. At the centre there is a stretch of open green sward where a cross has been erected.

Mortain

This little town was the centre of the last, but terrible, German counter-attack, in an effort to stop the advance of the American armies. Operation Lüttich, which Hitler wanted against the advice of von Kluge, the successor of von Rundstedt, who would have preferred to withdraw towards the Seine, involved launching a counter-attack on August 7th with eight of the nine armoured divi-

Patton monument at Avranches.

American cemetery
at Saint-James.

sions stationed in Normandy. The Germans managed to recapture Saint-Jean-du-Corail, but failed when they reached Barenton. The following day, between Gathemo and Saint-Barthéle-my, the fighter bombers of the Royal Air Force attacked the German tanks. General Barton's 4th division resisted before taking them in a pincer movement, recapturing Saint-Jean-du-Corail on August 11th. Mortain collapsed under repeated bombing, especially that of August 12th by the Luftwaffe, the day it was liberated after hand-to-hand fighting in the ruins of the town. Just like the other communes of the Mortain region, it was 84% destroyed.

The taking of Mortain marked the complete liberation of the Manche département. But a heavy price was paid: the deaths of thousands of civilians, plus soldiers, Americans and Germans. The "war of the hedges" ended with more than 12,000 dead. When Operation Cobra was launched, the elite German armoured division, the Panzer Lehr, lost more than 1,000 men in two days. The carpet bombing technique from more than 3,000 planes, allowed the Allies to take the initiative. Operation Cobra started on July 25th and allowed the American armies to reach Avranches on the 30th. General Patton, commanding the 3rd army, quickly took advantage of the breakthrough of the 1st American army.

Memorial chapel at Saint-James.

91

Cherbourg

At the north of the Cotentin peninsula, Cherbourg was placed in a wide gulf barred by a huge dyke separating a vast artificial roadstead. The American troops who landed on Utah Beach on June 6th had the mission of taking Cherbourg within ten days. But their advance was halted by fierce German resistance behind the woodland hedges and in front of each town or village on the way to Cherbourg. Each position had to be taken after fierce fighting. The American general staff brought in the 82nd airborne division, and the 4th, 9th, 79th and 90th infantry divisions. Their progress was extremely difficult, taking Chef-du-Pont on June 10th, Pont-l'Abbé on June 13th, Orglandes, Néhou, Saint-Sauveur-le-Vicomte on June 17th, and Saint-Jacques-de-Néhou and Barneville on June 18th. At this moment, the Cotentin peninsula was cut in two; General Collins led his offensive with his usual energy and installed thirty battalions.

Valognes

The little "Normandy Versailles" was bombed for three consecutive days; the 6th, 7th and 8th June. Many old town-houses were hit and the town was 75% destroyed. When Valognes was liberated on June 20th, the American soldiers of the 8th infantry division of Colonel Van Fleet entered a town in ruins and abandoned by its survivors.

Before this, they had launched an offensive on Orglandes in order to isolate the north of the Cotentin peninsula. The fighting lasted from June 15th to 17th, which demonstrates the ferocity of the German resistance. There is a German cemetery near this village, with 10,152 graves. The German soldiers who fell during the Cotentin fighting lie here. Their names are inscribed on the small stone crosses set in the green sward.

Left page:
American soldiers regarding the town of Cherbourg from the heights of Fort du Roule.

Ruins of Valognes.

Saint-Sauveur-le-Vicomte in ruins. Painting by Pierre Campain, 1946.

Montebourg

There is a local saying: "Who holds Montebourg holds Cherbourg". There were terrible combats between American and German troops there. The town was bombed on June 6th and most heavily on June 8th. After these bombardments the American soldiers attacked the town on June 12th. Fierce German resistance meant that the assaults had to be repeated in the following days. The town changed hands several times before being finally liberated at 3 a.m. on June 19th. On June 15th, stopped in front of Montebourg, General Joseph Lawton Collins stated that the *"main aim now of the army corps must be to cut off the peninsula"*. This aim was fulfilled on June 18th. After that, progress was rapid: the 19 miles between Bricquebec and Les Pieux took two days. The American troops advanced towards the west via Nehou and towards the south via Saint-Sauveur-le-Vicomte, which had been 75% destroyed.

The taking of La Haye-du-Puits on July 9th had been particularly deadly and was called "Bloody Hill". The attack against Mont Castre on July 8th resulted in the death of 2,000 soldiers. Once the Montebourg blockage had been breached, the doors to the Val de Saire opened. On June 20th in the evening, the troops of General Manton Eddy arrived at Cherbourg, ready to take the port, if necessary for the operations.

The Val de Saire comprised various defensive installations such as the La Pernelle batteries. These batteries, established on a peak 410 feet high, and equipped with 170 mm cannons with a range of 19 miles, covered the whole naval horizon from the La Hague cape to Utah Beach. On June 6th, Allied planes dropped 668 tons of bombs. The Germans did not want the cannons to fall into the hands of the Americans and destroyed them themselves on June 19th. The equipment of the radar station at Saint-Pierre-Eglise remained intact. It was protected by the most powerful battery on the Cotentin peninsula, the Hamburg battery equipped with four cannons of 240 mm. On June 25th an Anglo-Ame-

General Joseph Lawton Collins (1896-1987)

General Collins.

Joseph Lawton Collins was nicknamed "Lightning Joe" because of the rapidity of his action in the Pacific Ocean against the Japanese. He graduated from West Point in 1917, and arrived in Europe the same year. He was then part of the occupation troops in Germany. He was promoted General in 1942, and commanded the 25th division at Guadalcanal. In December 1943, he was sent to Great Britain. He commanded the 7th army corps at Utah Beach. He took Cherbourg, and this excellent tactician drew up Operation Cobra. He was a dedicated military chief, and took the 7th army corps as far as the Elbe, and then discovered the concentration camps. He became spokesman of the Ministry of Defence, and then Chief of Staff of the armies from 1949 to 1953. In 1954 he was named Ambassador to South Vietnam, but retired in 1956.

rican naval force attacked, but an air attack on June 28th was needed before the Germans surrendered. The Germans had planned to set up a V 1 site at Hardinvast, to send 1/2 ton bombs over the south of England, but they did not have the time to build the metallic ramp. About twenty ramps were built in North Cotentin, but they were quickly detected by the French resistance, bombed and put out of action.

Cherbourg

On June 19th, three American units, the 4th, 9th and 79th infantry divisions, commanded by General Joseph Lawton Collins, guided by resistants from Cherbourg, launched the attack on Cherbourg. At the same time, the Germans began the systematic destruction of Cherbourg's port installations. The Hommet jetty was blown up on June 19th, on the 20th the forward port blew up, while ships were scuttled in the channels and the whole port mined. On June 21st, General von Schlieben refused an offer of surrender.

The real battle of Cherbourg began on June 22nd with a massive air and naval pounding and continued with the encircling of the Cherbourg fortress. On the 23rd, the maritime terminal was dynamited by the German army whereas the Americans arrived in Tourlaville and encircled Equeurdreville. On the 24th, American pressure became so heavy that the Germans abandoned their destruction of the port. The final attack began on June 25th with a naval

bombardment of the German defences. The 4th and 79th American divisions occupied the east of the town. In the evening of the 25th, General Collins gave an ultimatum to General von Schlieben. On the 26th, the American soldiers took over every quarter of the town of Cherbourg. By the end of the day, the town had been liberated. Admiral Henneke and General von Schlieben, who had been ordered by Hitler and Rommel to resist until the very last bullet, gave themselves up from their underground bunker outside Octeville. Ten thousand soldiers were taken prisoner with them. The official capitulation was signed at Servigny castle, on the commune of Yvetot-Bocage, where General Collins had his command post. The arsenal, the Maupertuis airstrip and the forts on the main dyke fell in the following days. The whole of the north of the Cotentin peninsula was completely liberated by July 1st.

On June 27th, in the town hall, General Collins solemnly handed over to the mayor a French flag made out of parachute material. The huge losses of the 7th corps are evidence of the violence of the fighting: 2,800 dead, 3,000 missing and 13,500 wounded.

The Air Courrier, July 5th 1944: Cherbourg liberated.

Port of Cherbourg,
arrival of equipment and material
to supply the front.

When the 7th army corps took possession of Cherbourg, it discovered that the port had been completely devastated, obstructed by about a hundred wrecked ships and infested with mines. The quays had been destroyed, the arsenal ruined, and the sluicegates sabotaged. The first ship able to enter the port was a British mine sweeper. And with it, a flotilla of American, Canadian and English minesweepers, frogmen from the Royal Navy and divers systematically cleared the roadstead. They found every type of mine existing at that time: depression, magnetic or acoustic. Next the wrecks had to be re-floated. The port installations were roughly put back into working order in the record time of fifteen days, which is illustrated by the motto of the 333rd American engineers regiment: *"We do what is difficult immediately; the impossible takes a little longer".* However, it needed three months of tireless work, day and night, to open up the port of Cherbourg completely.

On July 16th, the first four Liberty ships entered the port. Cherbourg could take its place as the port the Americans needed to disembark their equipment, material and supplies necessary for continuing operations in the Cotentin peninsula, which Gilles Perrault called *"the central nourishing artery of the Allied armies".* On September 7th, 23,000 soldiers from the United States disembarked. Beginning from October 15th, over 20,000 tons of equipment and supplies were unloaded daily. On November 2nd, with 133 posts available on the quay, Cherbourg became the biggest port in the world with 1 million tons, before reaching 2 million tons in February 1945.

These figures demonstrate Cherbourg's strategic importance at the heart of the Allied organisation. Evacuation was carried out rapidly by railways which had been quickly repaired: from August 30th, the Cherbourg-Paris line was reopened, including lorries if necessary. From August 25th the

front was supplied following the "Red Ball Express Highway", a route leaving Saint-Lô to end up eventually in Brussels. According to the expression of Robert Lerouvillois, it was *«the longest one-way track ever put into service in the world»*. Its maximum length was 1,500 miles there and back and it carried 410,000 tons of supplies in three months. From Cherbourg to Saint-Lô, this track joined the Liberty Track. Cherbourg also sheltered hospital ships, and embarked 148,000 wounded.

*Traffic controller
on the Red Ball Express Highway.*

Querqueville, a town in the Cherbourg built-up area, was the terminal of the PLUTO pipeline from the Isle of Wight, 70 miles away.

It was the first under-water pipeline in history, and the idea came from Lord Louis Mountbatten. From August 12th, it supplied the armies with fuel. It was tried out in the Severn estuary, between Swansea and Ilfracombe, but unsuccessfully. A second was put into operation on August 21st. On November 30th, it carried 1 million litres of fuel per day. The pipeline followed the progress of the armies as far as Dourdan. Later it was named the "Major system" and linked up to Germany.

Roule mount

The Roule mount dominates the Cherbourg area at a height of 360 ft. Robert Lerouvillois quotes an old saying illustrating the strategic importance of this hill: *"He who holds Roule holds Cherbourg"*. The fort, built in the XIXth century, was equipped with a battery of four 105 mm cannons. By pointing their guns along the flank of the cliff at a height of 265 ft, they had a range of 7 1/2 miles. Despite the bombing, the fort resisted. It needed the courage of Corporal Kelly, ranger from the 314th infantry regiment, climbing up the rocks, to place explosive charges inside the blockhouse and thus get the Germans to surrender. Lieutenant Ogden, who was just as courageous, and belonging to the same division, advanced alone towards the German positions and

destroyed them with hand grenades. After two days of fierce and bloody fighting, the Americans controlled the Roule mount, at 9.48 p.m. on June 25th, and planted their flag there.

These days, the fort houses the Cherbourg Liberation Museum, the first museum depicting the Battle of

Fort on Roule mount.

PLUTO pipeline.

Normandy. It recalls the black years when France was occupied between 1940 and 1944 without showing any weapons or uniforms.

Three weeks after the landings on Utah Beach, the aim of the American armies had been achieved, with the capture of Cherbourg. The liberation of the north of the Cotentin peninsula provided the Allies with a dependable base, and installed them definitively on the continent so that they could continue their operations to liberate the south of the Manche département. But the American armies paid a high price for their progress since their landing on Utah Beach: 22,000 dead, wounded or missing.

The   Battle   for   Caen

The aim of the landings was to capture the city of Caen in the evening of June 6th, but the British armies did not manage to reach the capital of Lower Normandy. General Montgomery's troops were stopped to the north-west and west of Caen by solid German resistance on the Périers ridge and on the main road leading from Caen to Bayeux: forty tanks from the 21st Panzerdivision had taken up positions there. The young fanatics of the 12th SS Panzerdivision "Hitlerjugend", led by Colonel Kurt Meyer, a convinced Nazi, arrived from their base near Evreux and managed to take up position to the north of the city. The Allied armies attacked again on June 25th by a movement intended to encircle Caen from the south. In order to do this, they had to cross the rivers Odon and Orne and the battle cost them over 7,000 dead. Operation Epsom was stopped on July 1st since it had brought in the major part of the German armoured divisions but not captured Caen.

Caen

On June 6th, in Caen, at 2 o'clock in the morning, the 1,020th alert since the beginning of the Occupation sounded. This alert seemed as if it would never end, writes the deputy mayor of Caen, Joseph Poirier. During the violent bombing of June 6th and 7th, the centre of the city was destroyed and burned. Kurt Meyer, SS commander of the "Hitlerjugend", noted on June 7th: *"Caen is a sea of flames where civilians are wandering around in the ruins and the streets are blocked by rubble; it is almost impossible to breathe... From a military point of view, the destruction of Caen is an unspeakable folly"*. But these same SS who criticised the destruction of Caen had themselves committed an unspeakable crime, shooting 70 to 75 prisoners in the prison yards at 10.30 a.m. on the day of the landings. Their bodies were never found. On June 8th, more than 4,500 inhabitants of Caen took refuge in the Malherbe lycée and the Abbaye aux Hommes. The Bonsauver home and the refectory of the abbey were transformed into a hospital. The whole grouping, which had become a sanitary refuge, was miraculously spared.

Left page:
Saint-Pierre church *in the middle of the ruins.*

Refugees in the cloister *of the Abbaye aux Hommes.*

Montgomery on the cover of Time *magazine.*

Bernard Montgomery (1887-1976)

*He was wounded
in the First World War.
On November 2nd 1942 he was put
in command of the 8th British
army, and defeated Rommel
at El Alamein and the Axis armies
in Tunisia in May 1943.
He next took part in the campaigns
in Italy and Sicily.
In January 1944
he became second-in-command
to Eisenhower and modified
the Overlord project.*

*His armies fought fiercely
to take Caen,
and at a certain time
his authoritarianism
was disputed by his subordinates.
He was promoted Field Marshal
on August 31st 1944.
He commanded
the British armies and several
American divisions until the end
of the war. From 1951 to 1958,
he commanded the Atlantic forces
in Europe.*

Two weeks later, their numbers had doubled. The bombing continued with the same violence, in particular on June 13th and 14th. Back in the month of April, General Montgomery had warned that if the Germans reached Caen before him the city would be bombed: *"If the enemy reaches Caen before us and if its defences turn out to be too strong for us to capture the city on D-Day, Caen will be pounded by our bombers so that it cannot be of use to the enemy".*

Throughout the month of June, the assaults of the British army failed against a city which had been two-thirds destroyed. On July 7th, the city was violently attacked again: 450 Lancaster and Halifax bombers commanded by General Harris dropped over 2,500 tons of bombs on the northern part of Caen in less than one hour. Was this really necessary? For Alexander McKee: *"The 2,500 tons dropped from the air had no noticeable effect. If the British chiefs of staff had thought they could intimidate the Germans by killing French people, they made a huge error".* It was a massacre for nothing, decided by General Montgomery. Eisenhower began to talk about a British set-back and Montgomery, after several failures attacking Caen, decided to carry out this bombing on July 7th. No doubt "Monty" had a bad conscience about it, since there is no mention of it in his Memoirs.

By now, three-quarters of the city of Caen had been destroyed. One hundred and fifteen thousand British and Canadian soldiers launched yet another attack and after two days of fierce fighting, on Sunday July 9th at 6 p.m. the Canadian soldiers made a breakthrough to the right bank. But all the bridges over the river Orne had been destroyed by the Germans. The left bank, where the German soldiers of the 12th SS Panzerdivision and 272nd infantry division were established, was only liberated ten days later. But 35,000 inhabitants of Caen were disaster victims. The taking of Caen marked the end of Operation Charnwood carried out by the 21st British armies group.

The Memorial for Peace, built on the site of the command post of General Wilhelm Richter who led the 716th infantry division, reminds the visitor of the complete history of the XXth century. This post, installed in a chalk quarry, was entirely underground and closed by armour-plated doors. It contained the administrative services of the 716th division, a map room, a radio station, a telephone exchange, and various other technical installations. The memorial, built on the initiative of the City Council of Caen, was inaugurated on June 6th 1988 by the President of the Republic François Mitterrand and by the eleven ambassadors of the countries which fought for peace in 1944. On the facade of the building which is built in Caen stone, the following phrase is engraved on either side of the entrance: *"Pain broke me, brotherhood raised me up, a river of freedom flowed from my wound"*.

The Memorial leads the visitor along a well-studied historical route, divided into three different spaces, and helps him understand the political and strategic stakes of the XXth century. This museographic journey is illustrated by three audio-visual

Hall of the Caen memorial.

The Caen memorial seen from the Eisenhower Esplanade.

sections offering two films and an animated map of the Battle of Normandy. Its pacific intentions are affirmed by a gallery of Nobel Peace Prize winners. The International Park for the liberation of Europe, with its American and Canadian gardens, is dedicated to the Allied countries.

Ruin in the main road of Carpiquet.

Carpiquet

In 1941, the Germans built a concrete runway 1,000 yards long, to facilitate the movements of their planes. Two young Caennais, Jean Hébert and Denys Boudard, stole a German plane from here and flew to England. Because of its military and strategic interest, this aerodrome was one of the objectives of the Allied armies on June 6th. It was a failure, just like Caen. On June 18th, the aerodrome became one of the objectives of Operation Epsom which was only launched on June 25th, since it was delayed by the destruction of the artificial port of Vierville-sur-Mer. The aerodrome of Carpiquet was especially

Carpiquet airfield under German bombardment. Water-colour by Canadian Captain O. N. Fisher, July 12th 1944.

well defended by blockhouses in reinforced concrete, turrets equipped with machine guns, pillboxes linked by underground passages, anti-tank cannons of 75 mm and anti-aircraft guns of 50 mm. The whole ensemble was surrounded by many mines and lines of barbed wire. The commune was also defended by cannons and machine guns. The complexity and extent of these defences were known to the Canadian soldiers thanks to intelligence from the French resistance. The objective was assigned to the 5,000 men of the 8th Canadian brigade of the Royal Winnipeg Rifles and the tanks of Fort Garry Horse. From July 4th to 7th, Canadian soldiers and young fanatics from the 12th SS Panzerdivision "Hitlerjugend" took part in furious combats, often hand-to-hand, to take the airfield. The attack was launched at dawn on July 4th and the battle continued under a hail of shells fired from both sides. The first assault cost the 8th Canadian brigade 477 dead! Even though they came under a deluge of artillery and mortar fire, the Canadians managed to hold their position and push back German counter-attacks. On July 7th, however, the situation seemed to be impossible, since the numbers of dead and wounded were rising endlessly. This hell lasted until July 9th. Finally, some positions were taken by flame-throwers.

105

Ardenne Abbey nowadays.

Ardenne Abbey

The Canadian soldiers took the communes of Buron and Authie on June 7th, but had to repulse two SS attacks before giving up. Ardenne Abbey, about 1/2 mile from Carpiquet, stands in a strategic position overlooking Caen. This abbey, founded in the 12th century by Prémontré monks, had been fortified by the Todt organisation by installing pillboxes, and served as base for the German counter-attack against the Canadian soldiers, from June 7th. The combats to take this site were especially bitter because of the assassination of 18 Canadian soldiers by the young SS fanatics of the 12th Hitlerjugend under Kurt Meyer. The latter directed the movements of his tanks by coming and going on motorbike. The Abbey was liberated on July 9th during Operation Charnwood. The commune of Authie was liberated the same day after bloody fighting between Canadian and SS soldiers. The crime of the Ardenne abbey was unfortunately not the only one to be committed against prisoners: on June 8th, 48 Canadian soldiers of the Queen's Own Rifles from Toronto had been shot by the Germans.

There is a small chapel in memory of the Canadian soldiers. It comprises a wooden cross with a niche containing a statue of the Virgin Mary. A Canadian army steel helmet is suspended from the cross. The children of Authie bring flowers to this chapel every year.

Tourville-sur-Odon

This commune remains one of the most important places of the battle of the Odon during Operation Epsom launched by Marshal Montgomery with 60,000 men, 600 tanks and 700 cannons. The river Odon flows in a deep and narrow wooded valley, which makes it very difficult to cross. The attacks launched in an attempt to cross the Odon caused heavy losses among the British ranks. The 15th Scottish infantry division liberated this village on June 27th.

Spot height 112

This excellent observation point overlooking Caen was of great strategic importance. This sector was defined to the south by the valley of the Orne and to the north by the river Odon. The battle of the Odon took place at its foot. On June 25th everything began by a barrage of fire from land and sea in order to prepare the attack of the 15th Scottish infantry division. Its progress in the mud and under the rain was made even more difficult by the fierce resistance of the Hitlerjugend. On June 26th the Tourmauville bridge was taken, which allowed the 11th British armoured division to launch an attack on the hill. But they were pushed back by the 1st SS Panzer. The Germans regrouped three tank divisions along a line from Gavrus to Cheux and attacked in their turn, but without success. The fighting continued for nearly a month. On July 10th, the British made another attempt to cross the Odon, but were halted by the German defences. The Duke of Cornwall light infantry finally managed to cross on August 4th, but at the price of 2,000 dead. The hill changed hands ten times.

There is a monument at the crossroads of the D8 and D36, which pays homage to the Dorset and Hampshire battalions which were decimated during an attack launched from the Fontaine-Etoupefour castle by the Waffen SS.

Bourguébus

This commune was the framework of Operation Goodwood, launched on July 18th. The conquest of the ridge dominating this commune involved violent combats between British and German troops. The attack had been prepared by heavy bombing from 4,500 planes which pounded the sector for three hours. The British sent in three armoured divisions including the "Desert Rats", but were pushed back by three German armoured divisions: Tigers and Panthers against Sherman and Cromwell tanks, which still remains the greatest tank-fight of the Battle of Normandy. The 7th British armoured division arrived at Bourguébus on July 20th. The same day, Montgomery stopped Operation Goodwood which had cost too many men - 6,000 - too much equipment - 400 tanks - just to progress 7 miles. Like all the villages around, Bourguébus was hit and destroyed to a large extent.

Tilly-sur-Seulles

Norey-en-Bessin, a vital point, was captured at midday on June 7th by the Reginas and served as base for Operation Epsom. To the south, there is nowadays the British cemetery of Norrey-Saint-Manvieu. The battle of Tilly took place a few miles away. For eleven days, from June 8th to 19th, the 30th British army corps and the Panzer Lehr were locked in fierce combat. Arriving with 190 tanks, only 66 remained at the end of the clash. The German line of defence had held out, but at a great price! Apart from its tanks, the Panzer Lehr had lost

5,500 men. The commune changed hands twenty times and finally, on June 19th, was taken by the 50th British infantry division. At Tilly-sur-Seulles there is a cemetery with 1,224 graves as well as a museum which explains the battle. Not far away, the little hamlet of Jérusalem, in the Chouain commune, shelters 46 graves of British soldiers, including that of soldier Banks, only 16 years old!

The end of the battle of Caen and the entry of the British armies into the plain pushed the Germans back towards Falaise and the south of the Calvados département, where the Battle of Normandy ended. The Epsom and Goodwood operations played their part in these decisive advances.

Bourguébus church, 1944.

Rocquancourt church, 1944.

The copses and pastures of Calvados

On July 25th, parallel to Operation Cobra launched by the American troops in the south and centre of the Manche département, and as a back-up, General Montgomery launched Operation Bluecoat from Caumont-l'Eventé on July 30th in the direction of Montpinçon and Vire. Two British army corps, the 8th and the 30th, had the respective missions to take Bény-Bocage and Saint-Martin-des-Besaces, before advancing towards Vassy. The British breakthrough in the bocage took the German counter-attack by surprise at Mortain and the battle of Falaise-Chambois began.

Saint-Martin-des-Besaces

This commune was located at the limit of the British and American sectors. It was encircled on July 30th and liberated on the 31st at 11 a.m. by the 11th British armoured division. The "Breakthrough in the bocage" museum tells the history of the British soldiers and resistants who took part in liberating the bocage.

Villers-Bocage

The 7th British armoured division and the Panzer Lehr faced each other on June 13th. When a leading English tank came into the village, it was blown up by fire from the Tiger tank of SS Captain Michael Wittmann. He then knocked out the major part of the British tank columns: "the Desert Rats" were thus forced to withdraw, abandoning 25 tanks. This ace of tank combat, also responsible for the hangings of Tulle, could count 138 victories by the beginning of August. On August 8th he was killed near Cintheaux. The British 7th armoured division, more used to desert conditions and rapid movements, reacted badly to the woodlands of the local terrain. After the war, it was severely criticised by General Dempsey : "*The 7th armoured division, relying on its reputation, carried out this battle dishonourably*". At least this episode persuaded the German tanks to move away from the Cotentin fighting.

During the night of June 14th to 15th, Villers-Bocage was heavily bombed in order to prevent the regrouping of German tanks. On June 30th, a

German tanks in Villers-Bocage.

Aunay-sur-Odon in ruins. Drawing by Anthony Gross, August 13th 1944.

new and terrible bombing flattened this little town, which had been already liberated on August 4th by the Northumbrians.

Aunay-sur-Odon

This town is also a cross-roads and therefore was completely destroyed by aerial bombing: first of all on June 12th at 7 a.m. and then later between June 12th and 15th. Two hundred inhabitants were killed among the ruins during Operation Epsom facing the first tank battle between the 7th armoured division and the 10th SS

Aerial view of Vire bombarded.

Panzerdivision. The flattened town was liberated on August 5th by the 8th British army corps.

Not far away, in the little commune of Saint-Charles-de-Percy, there is a cemetery sheltering 792 graves of British soldiers.

Mont Pincon

This hill, 1,180 ft high, is steep and sharp. The foot-soldiers assaulted it on August 6th about midday from the western slope. They came under intense fire from the German defenders. Six tanks managed to reach the summit and were quickly backed up by foot-soldiers from the 4th Wiltshire regiment. It was very difficult for them to climb under the sun and through the bushes. This battle attracted the attention of the 1st and 9th Panzerdivisions, which weakened German forces around Caen.

Vire

This sub-prefecture was a road communications centre between the south and the west. As a result of its position, Vire was almost totally flattened by British bombing. On June 6th, the centre and main cross-roads Caen-Rennes and Paris-Granville were destroyed. The incessant bombing destroyed the town and its inhabitants fled.

The American soldiers had to conquer the hills overlooking Vire one by one. Two days of fierce fighting began on August 5th between the 29th American infantry division and the 2nd SS Panzer. After street fighting the town was liberated on August 7th. At the same time, Mont Pinçon was taken, but with difficulty. The last Germans left on August 8th, and the Allies witnessed that the town had been completely burned down and left in ruins: not only by their own bombing but mainly by the violence from the Germans.

Operation Bluecoat liberated the Calvados Bocage, but only at the price of very heavy destruction, with most of the communes being flattened. The woodlands and pastures, with their uplands and downlands, prevented concerted manoeuvres and the fighting continued until mid-August. Thury-Harcourt was only liberated on August 13th and Condé-sur-Noireau on August 17th.

The Vire bocage today.

The   Pocket

The whole plain between Caen and Falaise was a huge battlefield. On July 7th, the 1st Canadian army, commanded by Lieutenant-General Henry Crerar, launched an attack to the south which resulted in bloody fighting along the old D158 road. This battle ended with the Canadian soldiers taking Falaise on August 16th and 17th. The British and American armies, supported by Polish and French divisions, engaged in the last big battle for Normandy by encircling about 110,000 German soldiers in the Chambois Pocket.

Cintheaux-Langannerie

These two communes, liberated on August 8th and 9th, shelter two cemeteries. Near Cintheaux, on August 8th, Captain Michael Wittman was killed, and his Tiger tank was not found again before 1982.

Left page:
Canadian patrol in the ruins of Falaise.

Polish cemetery at Langannerie.

Canadian cemetery at Cintheaux.

Langannerie shelters the only Polish cemetery of the battle of Normandy, with 650 graves from the 1st Polish armoured division commanded by General Maczek. They were equipped with Sherman tanks involved for the first time in the battle of Normandy.

Cintheaux shelters one of the two Canadian cemeteries in Normandy. Just outside the commune lie 2,959 soldiers.

Falaise

At the outlet of the Caen plain, this sub-prefecture became one of Normandy's martyred towns. It was 85% destroyed by a succession of bombings over a period of more than two months. On August 7th, the Canadians attacked along the Caen to Falaise road during Operation Totalize. They had advanced by 5 miles by the evening of August 8th. But after two days they had to give up at 7 miles from Falaise since the 35 tanks of the 12th SS Panzerdivision were so resistant. During the night of August 13th to 14th, Operation Tractable was launched: 700 bombers dropped 4,000 tons of bombs on a town which had al-

ready been hit hard during the weeks before. After fierce fighting to take over the hills overlooking the town, the battle to take the town began on August 16th. Two days of bitter fighting between the Canadian soldiers and SS were needed for complete liberation. On the morning of August 17th, the Canadian soldiers of the 6th brigade entered Falaise and the following day the Mont-Royal light infantry, backed up by flame-throwing tanks, evacuated the last Germans from the town.

The August 1944 museum tells the history of this battle and is remarkable for its vehicles on display, in particular an Opel NSU caterpillar, a Kubelwagen Volkswagen and an English Lloyd Carrier.

Above. **August 1944 museum at Falaise.**
Opposite: **Falaise and its castle nowadays.**

Mont Ormel Memorial.

Mont Ormel

This mount, 3 miles north of Chambois, is formed of two twinned hills at spot height 262, and was renamed "Maczuga" (many weapons) by the soldiers of the 1st Polish armoured division of General Maczek, who took it on August 19th. They established themselves there with 80 tanks and 1,500 men. This achievement enabled the Allies to control both sides of the Chambois to Vimoutiers road and especially to dominate the whole valley of the river Dives. However, the Polish

Commemorative Memorial and the keep of Chambois castle.

soldiers remained separated from their Canadian comrades by a little valley leading to Vimoutiers. The breach allowed several thousands of German soldiers to escape.

A monument dominates the whole region and the valley of the Dives; it recalls the events in the form of a high wall in light-coloured stone. A tank and an armoured car are set at spot height 262.

The Mont Ormel Memorial, overlooking a site of exceptional beauty, recounts the complete history of the Pocket and commemorates the bloody battles there. There is a *son et lumière* lasting seventeen minutes.

Chambois

This little village in the Orne, dominated by a XIIth century castle with a square keep, remains famous as the theatre of the last great battle for the liberation of Normandy. Chambois is located on the main road of the Dives valley. Allied hesitations meant that 100,000 German soldiers were able to regroup in this sector. The Allies surrounded them, with the Canadian and Polish armies to the north, the American armies and the 2nd French armoured division of General Leclerc to the south, and the British army to the west.

In the morning of August 18th, the Canadian 4th armoured division took Trun and Saint-Lambert. On August 19th, at 7.20 a.m. the Polish troops linked up with the 395th American infantry regiment, which made it possible to lock the Falaise-Chambois Pocket. The following day, the German troops tried to counter-attack, but were pushed back at the price of bloody fighting. The day after this, the German paratroopers managed to open a passage between Saint-Lambert and Coudehard: this passage became known as the "Corridor of Death". On August 21st, a deluge of fire from Spitfires, Typhoons and artillery rained down on the few square miles where the German soldiers were encircled. From the top of Mont Ormel the Poles defended this position fiercely and endlessly pounded the Germans who were trying to attack. The battle became a real carnage where men and animals perished. The Germans, who had run out of fuel, tried to flee on foot or on horseback in a gigantic scramble. Erich Braun, of the 2nd Panzerdivision, wrote later about what the German soldiers had had to endure: *"Everywhere there was the chaos of explosions and men calling for help, the dead with their faces twisted with suffering, officers and men in a state of shock, vehicles on fire and men screaming inside,*

soldiers who had gone mad crying, shouting, swearing or bursting into hysterical laughter, horses whinnying in terror, still attached to their shafts and struggling on the stumps of their back legs to try to escape". The Polish and American armies managed to rejoin the 2nd DB of General Leclerc and the 2nd British armoured division. This action closed up the Pocket and forced the Germans who had not managed to escape to surrender. At midday on August 21st 1944, the Battle of Normandy had been won. Over 10,000 German soldiers had been killed and 40,000 to 50,000 taken prisoner, but about the same number had escaped. The Allies also suffered heavy losses: thus, on the Mont Ormel hill, only 114 Polish soldiers out of 1,560 were still operational. The battlefields around were piled up with the bodies of men and animals and the stench was terrible because of the heat.

On August 23rd, General Eisenhower commented on the horror of this final battle: *"It was possible to walk for hundred of yards on nothing but human remains in a state of decomposition, in heavy silence in luxuriant countryside where all life had suddenly stopped"*.

The battle of the Falaise-Chambois Pocket had concluded the Battle of Normandy successfully for the Allied armies. It had also opened the way for the freeing of France, with the liberation of Paris on August 24th, that is three days after this defeat of the armies of the IIIrd Reich, the most bitter since the battle of Stalingrad.

Surrender of a German detachment at Saint-Lambert, August 19th 1944.

Violence of the fighting for the Falaise-Chambois Pocket

117

La Presse
CHERBOURGEOISE
PARIS
EST LIBÉRÉ
Après quatre jours de lutte,
les Forces françaises de l'Intérieur fortes de 50.000 hommes armés,
ont chassé les Allemands de la Capitale
PARIS! PARIS!

Epilogue

Throughout this journey along the beaches of the allied landings, but also inland in the countryside of Lower Normandy, each person at each moment can feel a deep emotion which still exists. These 50 miles of French coastline are marked for ever by these first steps towards the liberation of Europe. The cemeteries of the Second World War bear witness to this battle, which killed 90,000 Allied and German soldiers. Total losses (killed, missing, wounded, taken prisoner) reached more than 600,000 men (209,672 Allies and 393,689 Germans). Jean Compagnon emphasises that *"the extent of the German defeat was considerable, both in human and material terms"*. Apart from the loss of men, the armies of the IIIrd Reich lost 1,500 tanks, 2,000 cannons and 20,000 vehicles. Air and naval superiority weighted the balance in favour of the Allies, while the German foot soldiers proved to be much more effective than the allied soldiers in close combat. The landings of June 6th 1944 and the Battle of Normandy will for ever remain the decisive stages in the liberation of Europe and in the outcome of the Second World War.

Apart from this military reckoning, one must not forget the civilian casualties: between 15,000 and 20,000 dead, mostly as a result of the bombing. The majority of the cities had to be rebuilt: 120,000 buildings had been completely destroyed and 270,000 damaged. Lower Normandy paid a very heavy price for its liberation, but it was the key to the liberation of Europe. In May 1944, understanding the imminence of a landing in his département, the Prefect of Calvados wrote in his monthly report: *"No-one has any illusions about the ordeal of invasion awaiting our country, but it is the only solution"*. Despite this ordeal, the joy of the Normans to

Children smiling.

be delivered from the Nazi yoke, was immense. Everyone welcomed the liberators with limitless enthusiasm.

General Dwight Eisenhower drew this conclusion after the Battle of Normandy: *"Among the reasons for our victory, one must take into account not only the successes of our troops on the battlefields but also the care and foresight involved in the preparations for the landings. We owe the essential factors of our success to the meticulous care taken in the preparation and organisation, such as: the degree of surprise when the landings took place, sufficient quantities of equipment and material, and the organisation which governed the exploits of our supply intendance. It is true that we had hoped that the tactical developments of the first days would allow us to seize the south and south-east region of Caen which would have meant we could build airfields... and take advantage of our armoured power, but it is no less exact that, on the scale of our overall strategy, we attained the line we had set for ourselves for D + 90 two weeks earlier than this date... But, of all the factors contributing to our victory, the most important lies undoubtedly in the qualities of the soldiers, sailors and aviators of the united nations"*.

Opposite:
The calvados is brought out again.

119

The routes
Area of tl

A veritable open air museum, the Historical Area of the Battle of Normandy brings together all museums and places of interest and remembrance connected with D-Day and the ensuing offensive in the three départements of Calvados, Manche and Orne. Eight itineraries in chronological sequence clearly signposted "Normandy Terre-Liberté", enable the visitor to discover these history-packed places and follow the unfolding of this huge battle on which the outcome of the Second World War depended.

OVERLORD-THE ASSAULT

OVERLORD-L'ASSAUT

This route is designed to help you discover a great many places that marked 6th June 1944 in the Anglo-Canadian sector from the right bank of the Orne estuary to Bayeux.

The visitor will first cross the famous Pegasus Bridge at Bénouville, then carry on along the coast following the Sword, Juno and Gold landing beaches as far as Arromanches, and the Longues battery... finally reaching Bayeux, the first French town to be liberated.

Distance: 72 km (45 miles)

D-DAY - THE ONSLAUGHT

D-DAY-LE CHOC

Starting out from Bayeux, this route covers the entire length of the Omaha sector as far as Carentan. Taking in places like Colleville-sur-Mer and the Pointe du Hoc, it gives an idea of the violence of the battle and the scale of the American casualties which earned Omaha Beach the nickname "Bloody Omaha".

The route then follows the hard-fought advance of the American troops towards the town of Saint-Lô, badly scarred by intensive bombing raids, and then takes the visitor through the marshlands to Carentan where the linkup took place with the troops coming ashore at Utah Beach.

Distance: 130 km (81 miles)

through the Historical
Battle of Normandy

OBJECTIVE - A PORT

OBJECTIF-UN PORT

From Carentan to Cherbourg, this route lets you relive the parachute drop by the American 82nd and 101st airborne divisions around Sainte-Mère-Eglise and the landing on Utah Beach at Sainte-Marie-du-Mont. It then invites the visitor to move on to Cherbourg along the route taken by the Allies to cut off the Cotentin peninsula and capture the port of Cherbourg, a vital base for importing the equipment and supplies required for the operation to succeed.

Distance: 95 km (60 miles)

THE CONFRONTATION

L'AFFRONTEMENT

Starting out at Bénouville, this completes the "Overlord-L'Assaut" route and follows the extremely difficult advance and consolidation of their beachhead by the British and Canadian troops. Between Caen, not liberated until 9th July, and Vire (in early August), strategic towns like Caumont-l'Evente and Saint-Martin-des-Besaces... would be wiped out under Allied artillery fire and air attacks during Operation "Bluecoat" (breakthrough in the Bocage), with the aim of supporting the American offensive in the west.

Distance: 207 km (129 miles)

COBRA -THE BREAKOUT

COBRA-LA PERCEE

From Cherbourg to Avranches, the visitor follows the difficult progress of the Allied tanks under General Patton, as far as the tremendous breakout at Avranches, which was not liberated until 31st July.

The towns of La Haye-du-Puits, Périers and Coutances, and the battlefield of Mont Castre, La Chapelle-Enjuger and Roncey show with what extreme difficulty the fighting forces contrived to get round the German defences entrenched in Normandy.

Distance: 174 km (109 miles)

THE COUNTER-ATTACK

LA CONTRE-ATTAQUE

The decisive phase of the Battle of Normandy took place with the wide sweep from Avranches to Mortain, where a deadly counteroffensive put paid to German hopes of halting the Allied advance.

From Mortain, the route then takes the visitor to Alençon along the line either side of which the Anglo-Canadian forces, to the north, and the American forces, to the south, would gradually close the jaws on the German divisions.

Distance: 209 km (130 miles)

THE ENCIRCLEMENT

L'ENCERCLEMENT

This itinerary, from Alençon to L'Aigle, gives an idea of how the trap designed to encircle the German forces closed in from the south. After following the progress of the French 2nd armoured division and American units moving northwards, the visitor discovers the places where the bloody and decisive battles were fought for the Falaise-Chambois Pocket, before going on to L'Aigle, whose liberation opened up the road to the Seine for the Allied armies.

Distance: 162 km (101 miles)

THE OUTCOME

LE DENOUEMENT

This circuit covers the phase in which the Allied offensives converged towards what would be the most decisive battlefield of the whole Normandy campaign, the Falaise Pocket... It follows in the footsteps of the British, Canadian and Polish armies, heading due south in Operation "Totalize" to meet American and French (2nd armoured) troops who had achieved a breakthrough towards Alençon and were moving north to encircle the German army as it withdrew following its failure at Mortain.

Distance: 128 km (80 miles)

1941 -August: Newfoundland meeting
- September 28 •British raid on Luc-sur-Mer
                •British raid on Saint-Aubin-sur-Mer

1942 - January 18: British raid on Saint-Laurent-sur-Mer
- August 19: Operation Jubilee at Dieppe
- September 13: British raid on Sainte-Honorine-des-Pertes
- November 8: Landing in North Africa

1943 - January 24: Casablanca Conference
- May: Trident Conference in Washington
- July 10: Landing in Sicily
- August: Quebec Conference
- December: Eisenhower leads Operation Overlord

1944 - January: Landing at Anzio
- February: Montgomery revises Overlord
- May 17: Eisenhower sets the D-Day landing for Monday June 5th
- June 3: Boarding of the troops
- June 6: Landings on five beaches
0hr20: The 6th airborne at Pegasus Bridge
0hr30: (roughly) the 101st dropped over Sainte-Mère-Eglise
2hr30: Liberation of Ranville
The 82nd airborne parachuted over the Cotentin peninsula
4hr30: Liberation of Sainte-Mère-Eglise
4hr45: Otway occupies Merville
6hr30: Landing at Omaha Beach and Utah Beach
7hr10: The Rangers at the foot of the Pointe du Hoc
7hr30: Landing at Gold Beach and Sword Beach
8hr00: Landing of the 3rd Canadian division at Juno Beach
8hr30: The Green Berets at Riva Bella
9hr30: Liberation of Bernières-sur-Mer
11hr00: Liberation of Vierville-sur-Mer
13hr00: Liberation of Ouistreham, Saint-Laurent-sur-Mer
19hr00: The Longues-sur-Mer battery neutralised
Liberation of Saint-Aubin-sur-Mer, Mauvaines, Douvres-la-Delivrande, Bény-sur-Mer,
Anguerny, Tailleville, Courseulles-sur-Mer, Hermanville-sur-Mer, Graye-sur-Mer, Ver-
sur-Mer, Asnelles-sur-Mer, Arromanches-les-Bains, Sainte-Marie-du-Mont, Hiesville
- June 7: Liberation of Lion-sur-Mer, Luc-sur-Mer, Langrune-sur-Mer, Creully, Bayeux,
Sainte-Honorine-des-Pertes, Colleville-sur-Mer, Blosville
Storming the Pointe de la Percée radar station
- June 8: Liberation of Port-en-Bessin
- June 9: Liberation of Grandcamp-les-Bains, Isigny-sur-Mer, Chef-du-Pont
- June 12: Winston Churchill, Eisenhower arrive in Bayeux
Link-up of the American troops of the Omaha and Utah sectors
Liberation of Anfréville, Carentan
Storming of the Crisbecq battery
- June 13: Liberation of Bréville
- June 14: Arrival of General de Gaulle
- June 15: Liberation of Quinéville
- June 16 : Arrival of King George VIth

- June 18 : The Cotentin peninsula is cut in half
- June 19 : Liberation of Montebourg, Tilly-sur-Seulles

The artificial port of Vierville-sur-Mer is destroyed by the storm

- June 20 : Liberation of Valognes
- June 25 : Operation Epsom

PLUTO pipeline at Port-en-Bessin

- June 26 : Liberation of Cherbourg
- June 27 : Liberation of Tourville-sur-Odon
- July 6 : The taking of Carpiquet
- July 8 : Assault of mount Castre

Operation Charnwood

- July 9 : Liberation of La Haye-du-Puits, left-bank of Caen, Ardenne abbey
- July 16 : First Liberty ships in Cherbourg harbour
- July 18 : Liberation of Saint-Lô, Hérouvillette, Carpiquet airfield

Operation Goodwood

- July 19 : Liberation of the right bank of Caen
- July 20 : The British in Bourguébus

Operation Cobra

- July 27 : Liberation of Marigny, Périers
- July 28 : Liberation of Coutances
- July 30 : Liberation of Avranches

Operation Bluecoat

- July 31 : Liberation of Granville
- August 1 : Leclerc and the 2nd armoured division land at Saint-Martin-de-Varreville
- August 1 : *Liberation of Saint-James*
- August 5 : Liberation of Aunay-sur-Odon
- August 7 : Liberation of Vire
- August 7 : Operation Totalize
- August 8 : Liberation of Cintheaux
- August 9 : Liberation of Langannerie

- August 12 : PLUTO pipeline in Cherbourg

Liberation of Mortain

2nd armoured division at Alencon

- August 14 : Operation Tractable
- August 15 : Landing in Provence
- August 17 : Liberation of Falaise, Troarn, Bures-les-Monts, Robehomme, Condé-sur-Noireau
- August 19 : Taking of Montormel
- August 21 : End of the Chambois battle
- August 22 : Liberation of L'Aigle
- August 23 : Liberation of Lisieux
- August 25 : Liberation of Paris

Kieffer enters Pont-l'Evéque

- September 12 : Liberation of Le Havre and end of the Battle of Normandy
- November 2 : Cherbourg is the world's leading port

"June 44" Museum at L'Aigle.

Monument at the
Leclerc Museum
in Alencon.

THE CEMETERIES OF THE SECOND WORLD WAR IN LOWER-NORMANDY

American
- Colleville-sur-Mer (Calvados) 9,386 graves, between Arromanches and Grandcamp
- Saint-James (Manche) 4,410 graves, between Avranches and Fougères

British
- Banneville-Sannerville (Calvados) 2,175 graves, between Caen and Troam
- Bayeux (Calvados) 4,648 graves including 466 German graves and other nationalities, including Russians
  1,807 names of missing on the Memorial
- Brouay (Calvados) 377 graves, between Caen and Bayeux
- Cambes-en-Plaine (Calvados) 224 graves, between Caen and Courseulles
- Chouain (Calvados) 40 graves, between Bayeux and Tilly-sur-Seulles
- Douvres-la-Délivrande, 927 graves and 182 German graves, between Caen and Luc-sur-Mer
- Fontenay-le-Pesnel (Calvados) 520 graves and 59 German graves, between Caen and Caumont-l'Eventé
- Hermanville-sur-Mer (Calvados) 986 graves, on the coast
- Hottot-les-Bagues (Calvados) 965 graves and 132 German graves, between Caen and Caumont-l'Eventé
- Ranville (Calvados) 2,151 graves and 323 German graves, near Pegasus Bridge
- Ryes-Bazenville (Calvados) 630 graves and 328 German graves, between Bayeux and Arromanches
- Saint-Manvieu-Norrey (Calvados) 2,186 graves, between Caen and Caumont-l'Eventé
- Secqueville-en-Bessin (Calvados) 117 graves and 18 German graves, between Caen and Bayeux
- Tilly-sur-Seulles (Calvados) 1,224 graves and 232 German graves, between Caen and Balleroy
- Saint-Charles-de-Percy (Calvados) 792 graves, near Bény-Bocage
- Saint-Désir-de-Lisieux (Calvados) 469 graves, near Lisieux

French
- Nécropole des Gateys (Orne), north of Alençon

Canadian
- Bény-sur-Mer-Reviers (Calvados) 2,043 graves, near Courseulles
- Cintheaux (Calvados) 2,958 graves, between Caen and Falaise

Polish
- Langannerie (Calvados) 650 graves, between Caen and Falaise

German
- La Cambe (Calvados) 21,160 graves, between Bayeux and Isigny
- Huisne-sur-Mer (Manche) 11,956 graves, near the Mont-Saint-Michel
- Marigny-La Chapelle-Enjuger (Manche) 11,169 graves, between Saint-Lô and Coutances
- Orglandes (Manche) 10,152 graves, south of Valognes
- Saint-Désir-de-Lisieux (Calvados) 3,735 graves, near Lisieux

ACKNOWLEDGEMENTS

I would like to thank Nathalie Worthington and Franck Marie
of the Caen Memorial, Stéphanie Martin from the Public Relations
and Communications department of the Town Hall of Cherbourg,
Christèle Collet of the Montormel Memorial, for their contribution,
and Monique for her careful rereading.

BIBLIOGRAPHY

Bataille de Normandie, Guides Gallimard, 1994.

BENAMOU (Jean-Pierre), BERNAGE (Georges) and LEJUEE (Philippe), *Pegasus Bridge 6ᵉ Airborne,* published by Heimdal, 1993.

BERNAGE (Georges), MCNAIR (Ronald) and LEJUEE (Philippe), *Le Couloir de la mort,* published by Heimdal, 1994.

BOUSSEL (Patrice) and FLORENTIN (Eddy), *Le Guide des plages du débarquement et des champs de bataille de Normandie,* published by Presses de la Cité, 1984.

COMPAGNON (Jean), *Les Plages du débarquement,* published by Ouest-France, 1979.

COMPAGNON (Jean), *6 juin 1944 - Débarquement en Normandie - Victoire stratégique de la guerre,* published by Ouest-France, 1984

DESQUESNES (Rémy), Sword Beach Ouistreham; Juno Beach Courseulles; Gold Beach Asnelles; Omaha Beach; Utah Beach, published by Ouest-France/Mémorial, 1989; *La préparation du débarquement en Normandie,* published by Ouest-France/Mémorial, 1990; *La Pointe du Hoc,* published by Ouest-France/Mémorial, 1992.

DESQUESNES (Rémy), *Normandie 1944,* published by Ouest-France/Mémorial, 1993.

DESQUESNES (Rémy) and BOURNIER (Isabelle), *La Batterie allemande de Longues-sur-Mer,* published by Mémorial, 1993.

HENRY (Jacques), *La Normandie en flammes,* published by Corlet, 1984.

FLORENTIN (Eddy) *Les 5 plages du 6 juin,* Guides Historia-Tallandier, 1988.

FLORENTIN (Eddy), *Stalingrad en Normandie,* published by Presses de la Cité, 1981.

Le Jour J et la bataille de Normandie 1944, Guide Pitkin, 1994.

KEMP (Anthony), *6 juin 1944 - Le débarquement allié en Normandie,* published by Gallimard/Découvertes, 1994.

LE CACHEUX (Geneviève) and QUELLIEN (Jean), *Le Dictionnaire de la libération du nord-ouest de la France,* published by Corlet, 1994.

LECOUTURIER (Yves), *Dictionnaire du Calvados occupé,* published by Paradigme, 1990.

LECOUTURIER (Yves), *La Situation en Basse-Normandie à la veille du débarquement.* Symposium *L'été 1944. Les Normands dans la bataille,* Archives of the Département of Calvados, 1994.

LE MARESQUIER (Augustin), *La Manche libérée et meurtrie,* published by Entr'aide française, 1946.

LEROUVILLOIS (Robert), *Et la liberté vint de Cherbourg,* published by Corlet, 1991.

McKEE (Alexander), *La Bataille de Caen,* published by Presses de la Cité, 1965.

MAN (John), *Atlas du débarquement et de la bataille de Normandie 6 juin - 24 août,* published by Autrement, 1994.

POIRIER (Joseph), *La Bataille de Caen,* published by Caron, 1945.

QUELLIEN (Jean), *La Normandie au cœur de la guerre,* Series Seconde Guerre Mondiale, published by Ouest-France/Mémorial, 1992.

RUPPENTHAL (Roland G.), *The European theater of operations logistical support of the armies.* Vol 1 May 1941 - Sep. 1944, Washington. OFF of the Chief of Military history, 1953.

RYAN (Cornélius), *Le Jour le plus long,* published by Robert Laffont, 1960.

Illustrations

Mémorial (U.S. Army, Coast Guard, E. Grunberg, J.-M. Piel, J. Blondel, Manuel Bromberg, Sean McDonald, O. N. Fisher, Abbé Hardy). Allen Jones. Patricia Canino. Yves Lecouturier. CDT Calvados (G. Rigoulet, O. Houdart). CDT Orne. Avranches Tourist Office. Cherbourg town hall. Mont-Ormel Memorial. Canadian Public Archives. Imperial War Museum. Bundesarchiv. Roger-Viollet. J.-L. Bourlet. Copyright: p. 84, 94 (t and b), 97.

Tourist information concerning
the Historical Area of the Battle of Normandy

Calvados Tourist Board
Place du Canada, 14000 Caen
Tel. + 33 (0)2 31 27 90 30 - Fax: + 33 (0)02 31 27 90 35 -
E-mail: calvatour@mail.cpod.fr

Manche Tourist Board
Maison du Département, 50008 Saint-Lô Cedex
Tel. + 33 (0)2 33 05 98 70 - Fax: + 33 (0)2 33 56 07 03

Orne Tourist Board
88 rue de Saint-Blaise - BP 50, 61002 Alençon Cedex
Tel. +33 (0)2 33 28 88 71 - Fax: + 33 (0)2 33 29 81 60 -
E-mail : orne.tourisme@wanadoo.fr

Normandy Tourist Board
Le Doyenné - 14 rue Charles-Corbeau, 27000 Evreux
Tél. : + 33 (0)2 32 33 94 00 - Fax : + 33 (0)2 32 31 19 04 -
E-mail : normandy@imaginet.fr - Internet : www.normandy-tourism.fr

CARTOGRAPHY
Patrick MÉRIENNE

GRAPHIC DESIGN
TERRE DE BRUME

© 1999 - ÉDILARGE S.A. - ÉDITIONS OUEST-FRANCE, RENNES
PHOTOGRAVURE SCANN'OUEST, RENNES
ACHEVÉ D'IMPRIMER EN JUILLET 1999, PAR MAME IMPRIMEURS, TOURS (N° 99072042)
ISBN : 2.7373.2388.6   N° ÉDITEUR : 3776.02.06.07.99
DÉPÔT LÉGAL : FÉVRIER 1999